101 Medical School Personal Statements
That Made a Difference

Dr. Nancy L. Nolan

Electronic and paperback versions published by:

Magnificent Milestones, Inc.
www.ivyleagueadmission.com

ISBN   9781933819631

<u>Disclaimers</u>:

(1) This book is a compilation of successful personal statements; it does not claim to be the definitive word on the subject of medical school admission. The opinions expressed are the personal observations of the author based on her own experiences. They are not intended to prejudice any party. Accordingly, the author and publisher do not accept any liability or responsibility for any loss or damage that have been caused, or alleged to have been caused, through the use of information in this book.

(2) Admission to medical school depends on several factors in addition to a candidate's personal statement (including GPA, MCAT scores, recommendation letters, and interview). The author and publisher cannot guarantee that any applicant will be admitted to any specific school or program if (s)he follows the information in this book.

Dedication

For students everywhere;
may the size of your dreams be exceeded only
by your tenacity to attain them.

Acknowledgements

I am deeply indebted to the students, professors, physicians and admissions officers who have shared their perceptions and frustrations about personal statements. This book, which was written on your behalf, would not be nearly as powerful without your generous and insightful input.

I also want to thank my colleagues at www.ivyleagueadmission.com for providing a constant source of support, along with the best editorial help in the business.

101 Medical School Personal Statements That Made a Difference

Table of Contents

Chapter 1: Introduction: The Medical School Admission Process

For most students, few processes are as daunting as applying to medical school. Competition is fierce at top programs, which receive hundreds of applications for every seat in the class. Due to the large volume of applications that they receive, most schools evaluate candidates on a two-step basis:

1. **The Numbers**. The primary screening is strictly the "numbers" that reveal your intellectual strengths. To gain admission to a specific medical school, your GPA and MCAT scores *must* exceed the minimum cutoff level that the school has imposed. Selectivity varies greatly among programs, which means that scores that are considered "great" at one school may not be competitive at another. As a general rule, successful candidates at state schools have a minimum GPA of 3.25 to 4.0 (out of a possible 4.0) and a minimum MCAT score of 27. At highly competitive programs, the cutoffs are as high as 3.75 and 33 for the GPA and MCAT, respectively. Candidates whose "numbers" fall below these levels can still gain admission in special circumstances, but their odds of success are greatly diminished.

2. **Personal Strengths**. Candidates whose "numbers" meet the school's expectations are further evaluated for their personal fit for their intended program. In the pre-interview stage, this "fit" is assessed from the applicant's personal statement and reference letters. Without exception, these documents *must* highlight the skills and traits that top schools covet, including honor, maturity, compassion, a solid work ethic and exemplary communication skills.

A great personal statement brings your "numbers" to life and provides a creative description of your performance and potential. It also provides critical information about your personality, ethics and integrity that isn't revealed anywhere elsewhere in your application. The BEST statements are short, specific and insightful. They are written by candidates who know what they want and aren't afraid to go for it.

Here is what the committee hopes to learn from your personal statement:

- Your unique qualifications, including the depth of your academic and extracurricular experiences
- Your personal traits and interests that aren't presented anywhere else in the application
- Your demonstrated commitment to pursuing a medical degree – and why you chose it
- How you compare to other candidates with similar aspirations

An effective personal statement should *supplement* the data you have provided the school about your academic and professional history, rather than duplicate it. Ideally, it will provide the reader with critical information about your personality, ethics and integrity that they couldn't uncover any other way.

The Importance of the Personal Statement in the Admissions Decision

The most common question we are asked about personal statements is how they are used in the admissions process. As a general rule, they supplement the primary admissions criteria, which are your GPA and MCAT score. In highly competitive programs, the applicant pool can quickly be sorted into three categories:

a. candidates with excellent grades and test scores: good chance of admission
b. candidates who are borderline cases: application is competitive, but not outstanding
c. candidates with low grades and disappointing test scores: poor chance of admission

Unfortunately, if you fall into category c, even a great personal statement may not save you from rejection. In a highly competitive applicant pool, schools usually screen out lesser qualified applicants by imposing a minimum "cutoff" for GPA and MCAT scores. Although a personal statement can "explain" a disappointing academic performance, it usually cannot compensate for it. There are limits to how much leeway a school will give to a candidate who does not present a solid track record of success.

In contrast, essays from candidates in category a are usually disaster checks. These applicants have exceptional grades, top test scores and persuasive letters of recommendation. On paper, they are everything a top school is looking for. Their personal statements must:

- explain their motivation and goals
- document their character, integrity and work ethic

For candidates in category a (excellent grades and test scores), a bad or mediocre personal statement can be extremely harmful. In a highly competitive applicant pool, each piece of the admissions puzzle (GPA, MCAT score, personal statement, reference letters, and personal interview) must "fit" together in a cohesive manner to show the committee who you are and what you have to offer. If your statement is poorly written, or reveals a lack of focus and dedication, the committee will be less likely to take a chance on you.

Surprisingly, nearly 70% of the applicant pool falls into category b, or borderline. These candidates have competitive grades and test scores, but are otherwise not distinguishable from others with similar "numbers." Their acceptance or rejection often hinges on an exceptional intrinsic quality that captures the committee's interest and makes a positive impression. In some cases, this can be their commitment to family, their dedication to community service or their ability to overcome an obstacle. A persuasive personal statement that discusses a candidate's passion (and how (s)he plans to use that skill in the future) can make or break his/her application; it provides the final piece of the "puzzle" that the committee needs to become excited about the applicant.

Writing Tips

In a typical day, a medical school admissions officer will read between 10 and 25 personal statements from candidates around the world. What makes a positive impression? Passion. Sincerity. Insight about yourself and the world around you.

From our experience, a great personal statement can take any number of forms; since no two candidates are alike, their personal statements won't be, either. Consequently, the only "magic formula" is honesty; you must have the courage to reveal your true personality, whatever that may be. Show the committee who you are and what you will bring to their program. Show them the contribution that only *you* can make.

We surveyed thirty admission officers on what they expect to see in a personal statement. Here's what works:

1. **Answer the question that was asked**. Tell us why you want to become a physician and why you believe you will be good at it. Show us that you have the maturity and insight to set and achieve realistic goals.

2. **Write naturally, but concisely**. Use simple sentences and your everyday vocabulary. Don't waste time on fancy introductions; get to the point quickly and reinforce it with specific examples.

3. **Use excellent grammar and punctuation**. Use logical paragraph breaks to separate your thoughts and to make the essay easier to read. Proofread your work carefully before you submit it. Don't let carelessness ruin your chances.

4. **Show your real personality (let us get to know you)**. Too many personal statements are long, boring theoretical pieces about medical research. No matter how well-written or researched, they don't tell us a darn thing about the candidate. Anyone can write a rational, detached paper, but that's not what we are looking for. We want to get to know you and the unique contribution you will make to our school.

5. **Personalize your essay as much as possible**. Write about your own unique, funny, interesting experiences. Provide details to add color. Adopt a relaxed, conversational style.

6. **Use humor only if it works**. Few people can write humorous prose or recount funny experiences effectively. If you have this gift, by all means use it. Before sending us a "funny" essay, though, have several people read your material to make sure it comes across well on paper. Avoid anything off-color or mean-spirited.

7. **Convey a positive message (avoid cynicism)**. Many applicants discuss a misfortune they have experienced and how it has shaped their personality. Be very careful of your tone if you decide to write about a hard-luck story. Avoid the "victimization" perspective; instead, focus on how you *overcame* the setback. Show us how the experience helped you to demonstrate your stamina, perseverance and intelligence. If written well, these essays show us that you can succeed in the face of terrible obstacles. If written badly, they will make you sound plaintive, self-righteous and bitter.

8. **Use the active voice**. Nothing is more tedious than trying to read a personal statement that was written in

the cold, detached passive voice. Although it is common in technical journals, it is pretentious and verbose in everyday writing. Keep your verbs simple and active. What's the difference?

Active Voice: The cow jumped over the moon.
Passive Voice: The moon was jumped over by the cow.

Yes, it sounds that silly when *you* use it, too!

9. **Explain events whenever appropriate**. The committee is interested in your accomplishments because of *why* you tackled them, what you thought about them and what you learned from the experience. Tell us the reasoning behind your decision and how your life changed as a result of it.

10. **Be specific and focused.** Rather than list several items or events, give a full description of just one. The more details you include, the more personal your statement will be.

11. **Proofread several times and get feedback from valued sources**. Explain to them what you hope to convey in your writing and ask them whether or not you met your objectives. The true test of your writing isn't what you *intended* to say, but what the reader actually understands.

12. **Revise and polish until it is perfect**. Give yourself enough time to do the statement well. Successful applicants usually invest several hours deciding the correct approach, constructing an outline and writing a first draft. You may have to write and revise multiple drafts before you are satisfied with your essay.

Common Pitfalls to Avoid

1. **Don't let anyone else tell you what to write**. Well-meaning parents and advisors often interfere in the writing process, which tends to sabotage the candidate's chances. Use your own best judgment in choosing a topic and writing your statement. Don't let anyone else influence you. We read thousands of essays each year, and have developed a keen eye for authenticity.

2. **Don't oversell yourself or try too hard**. Many candidates manage to squeeze every accomplishment they've ever had into a two-page personal statement. Others explain emphatically how much they "really, really" want to attend our school. Don't take such a desperate approach; just be yourself.

3. **Don't rehash information that can be found elsewhere in the application**. We already know your GPA, MCAT scores, academic awards and honors. Use your personal statement to discuss experiences that aren't revealed anywhere else. Consider your essay to be an informal interview, your exclusive "one-on-one" time with the committee. Show us why we should accept you into our academic community.

4. **Don't write a scholarly or technical paper on a specific legal case**. The personal statement is your only opportunity to demonstrate your non-academic strengths, particularly your personality. Don't waste it.

5. **Resist the urge to write a manipulative or argumentative essay on a controversial issue**. Be original. Each year, we receive hundreds of personal statements that discuss the horrors of managed care and the moral implications of stem cell research. Sadly, they don't tell us anything we don't already know. If you choose to discuss a meaningful issue, do so in the context of your demonstrated commitment to changing it, either through your career or volunteer work. Don't confuse passive idealism (or future intentions) with productive action. A demonstrated commitment to a cause is worth writing about; passive idealism is not.

6. **Don't try to explain academic blemishes in your primary statement**. With rare exceptions, it is impossible to explain poor grades and test scores without sounding irresponsible or defensive, which will not enhance your primary statement. If you have a compelling excuse for an academic disappointment, place it in a separate addendum to your file, rather than in the body of your personal statement.

7. **Don't use large, pretentious words**. Use the simplest language to explain your meaning precisely. Using three-dollar words to impress the committee usually backfires, because it comes across as presumptuous and arrogant.

8. **Don't be boring and safe; tell a real story!** A fresh and well-written personal statement will enhance your application.

9. **Don't lie or exaggerate.** Applicants seldom realize how easy it is to detect lies and half-truths in admissions essays. Don't pretend to be someone you are not. After reading your application, the committee will have an excellent "feel" for your character. Consequently, they will be able to sense if a reported event or achievement isn't consistent with the rest of your history. Lying is a fatal mistake. A single misrepresentation on your application will lead us to doubt all of your other assertions.

10. **Don't be gimmicky.** Avoid using definitions to begin your personal statement. This crutch was extremely popular in the late 90's, but is now synonymous with sloppy writing. Avoid using cute or "meaningful" quotations, unless they perfectly fit the character and tone of your essay. Quotations are terrific if they are seldom-quoted and deeply relevant to your chosen topic. All too often, though, their usage is cliche and the resulting essay is unimaginative.

11. **Don't play games with the word limit.** Don't use a miniscule type size or invisible border to shrink an essay to the stipulated length. Except in extreme circumstances, your finished statement should adhere to the maximum word limit. In many cases, less is more. Convey your points quickly and efficiently; don't feel obligated to "fill" extra space.

Strengths to Highlight

Your personal statement MUST emphasize the intrinsic traits that the committee seeks in the admissions process. Due to the high ethical standards and level of critical thinking that are expected in the medical profession, your character and motivation will be highly scrutinized by the selection committee. Use your primary statement and secondary essays to sell your *whole* self, not just the individual pieces that you think the school wants to see.

Admissions officers seek the following traits in medical school applicants:

Honesty	Creativity	Compassion
Logical Thinking	Independence	Confidence
Humor	Perseverance	Communication Skills
Objectivity	Maturity	Strong Personal Ethics

To whatever extent possible, you should build your essays around the achievements and experiences that have enabled you to cultivate and display these strengths. This is your only chance to sell yourself; use it for everything that it's worth.

The personal statements of successful applicants will probably surprise you. They are seldom academic in nature, and they may seem risky to candidates who feel compelled to assume a false (or misleading) persona for the committee's benefit. That's why studying these statements is so valuable. They reveal the heart and soul of each writer and demonstrate what (s)he would add to the medical school class.

These candidates were accepted because they caught the eye (and captured the heart) of a receptive admissions officer. They have accomplished what you are trying to do. Before you sit down to write your own personal statement, read on!

Chapter 2: Candidates with Medical Experience

Many candidates have experience in the medical profession through summer jobs, volunteer positions, and hospital internships, which provide an extraordinary chance for them to observe the daily realities of the profession. For these candidates, the personal statement is a golden opportunity to explain how their exposure to medicine has influenced their long-term goals.

Here are several excellent personal statements from candidates with volunteer experience who gained admission to highly competitive medical schools. To protect the privacy of the writer, the names of all people, classes, schools, places, teams, activities, and companies have been changed.

Volunteer Experience

Many times, I have wondered what I would say to my birth mother if I had the chance to meet her. After careful reflection, I am certain that I would simply express my thankfulness. By choosing adoption, my birth mother gave me the chance for a loving and secure future. My gratitude for her sacrifice – and for my family, friends, health and education, has inspired me to reach out to others who have not been similarly blessed.

With this in mind, I completed a mission trip to India, where I worked at the orphanage where I had been surrendered nearly two decades beforehand. The nuns who ran the facility were remarkable educators who provided exemplary care to more than one hundred orphaned children. With limited resources, they also taught local families how to introduce protein and vegetables into their diets by cultivating their own gardens. In a community plagued by poverty, obesity, and illiteracy, they provided a vital flow of health information to the people who needed it the most.

When I returned from India, I was determined to become a similar vehicle for change. To immerse myself in the needs of a developing country, I became a Peace Corps volunteer in Ghana. My primary job was to teach health and disease prevention to local children. In this poor nation, where many girls work as prostitutes, nearly one in three children is infected with HIV/AIDS. On several occasions, I saw my own students dressed provocatively at a local nightclub, surrounded by older men. In an instant, the statistics assumed a painful level of urgency; I was determined to do whatever I could to protect and educate my students.

In Ghana, numerous social ills fuel the AIDS epidemic, including poverty, alcoholism, and limited medical resources. In the absence of affordable treatment, few children are willing to be tested for HIV. To raise awareness about the virus, I launched a peer education program that employed the same methods that the nuns had used in India. By educating parents and teachers about HIV – and using them as messengers in the community, we provided education and support to previously unreachable neighborhoods. Eventually, this knowledge can serve as the catalyst for lasting change.

When I returned to Canada, I accepted a two-year position as a nurse practitioner at a tiny clinic in Nunavut, where I encountered the same obstacles to health care that I had observed in India and Ghana. In this poor rural area, few people could afford to see a doctor; even fewer had access to specialized care for hypertension, obesity, and diabetes. In the absence of preventive programs, residents frequently suffered severe and preventable medical complications. Throughout my two years in Nunavut, I solicited grants for a fitness and nutrition program to combat obesity and diabetes. I also used simple clinical measurements, such as grip strength, walking speed, and weight loss, to assess the frailty of our elderly patients. At the Nunavut Elderly Center, I trained our staff to conduct these tests as part of our regular clinical assessments. By providing the data to the physician, we increased the likelihood of obtaining the correct diagnosis – and cause – of a patient's condition.

Buoyed by these experiences, I decided to complete my Master's degree in public health at the University of San Diego, where I am exploring the effects of support networks in the lives of patients with HIV. As part of our study, we are collaborating with a primary care clinic at a local hospital, which offers an extraordinary chance to bridge the gap between clinical medicine and public health. The most riveting part of my work is interacting with patients, whose courage has touched my heart.

In recent months, I have pondered the best way to promote lasting change in medicine. At the University of San Diego, I have been privileged to work with many accomplished physicians who have provided their patients with great relief. Looking ahead, I would like to become a doctor who makes a similar difference in the lives of my own patients. My experiences in India, Ghana, and Nunavut have revealed a dire need for primary care physicians in underserved areas, where infectious diseases continue to proliferate. With my background in public health, a degree in medicine, and my passion to serve others, I can make a tangible difference in these communities – and in the lives of the patients who rely upon me.

<u>Our Assessment</u>: This candidate brought an impressive background in public health and international health care to medical school, which is reflected in his statement. His creative opening about adoption made a particular impression on the committee, because it explained his initial interest in volunteer work. No one else could have written this story, which is what made it so powerful and memorable.

Volunteer Experience

Since early childhood, I have been captivated by my father's inspirational stories of his career as a pediatrician. While practicing medicine in the same small town for 30 years, he became a friend and role model to every person I know. Ironically, I am actually more impressed by his second job at an inner city clinic nearly two hours from our home. Every weekend, my father and his staff provide free medical care to disadvantaged children who would not otherwise receive it. There, in his Spartan office with minimal resources, my father faces critical medical challenges that hone his skills as a clinician. After medical school, I hope to emulate his example by opening my own inner city practice.

Due to my parents' careers, I was privileged to grow up in an upscale rural area with numerous financial and educational resources. Although our world was safe and secure, my family also felt it was important for us to give back to our community. My parents encouraged my initial volunteer experiences, which later became my true passion. Thus, although others may judge me by my appearance, race, and socioeconomic status, I know in my heart that my true character has been shaped by the people I have met through volunteering.

In high school, my initial community service work was tutoring Spanish to a group of ESL (English as a Second Language) students in downtown Boston. As a second generation Mexican-American, I was eager to help recent immigrants cultivate their language skills, which would allow them to live successful and independent lives. On several occasions, my father told me about his terrible struggle to learn English and succeed in the classroom among native speakers of the language. I was honored to help other people overcome the same hurdle.

In my junior year, I accepted a volunteer position in the Coronary Care Unit of Boston Community Hospital, where I helped post-surgical patients eat, dress and move around the hospital. To me, the intimacy of this experience was thrilling; I witnessed their tentative first steps after open heart surgery and the joy of their recovery. I felt privileged to be taken into their confidence during one of the most stressful times of their lives. During awkward moments, I sometimes didn't know what to say. Later, I realized that nothing needed to be said; just being there as a caring and supportive presence was enough.

This past semester, I have volunteered as a counselor at the Hatfield General Clinic, where my father works on weekends. The clinic serves a poor inner city area that is miles away from the nearest public hospital. We have many emergencies, including shootings, stabbings and other results of gang violence. Some women use the clinic as their only source of prenatal care – one visit to confirm the pregnancy and the second to deliver the baby. Due to the variety of patients and the pace of the work, the excitement in the clinic is palpable. With limited funds, it sometimes feels like we are putting a Band-Aid on a volcano, yet we feel compelled to do whatever is necessary to help patients who have fallen through the cracks of the traditional health care system.

For my senior project, I developed an awareness program for childhood immunizations, including an informational brochure that we distributed at local Laundromats, grocery stores, restaurants and bars. I also offered an informal question and answer session to discuss the potential risks of the shots. At our seminars, my father and his staff patiently answer every question that is asked. Although we have not immunized everyone, we are certainly off to a good start. I believe this is how all change happens: one person at a time, one interaction at a time.

To prepare for medical school, I have completed a dual major in biology and chemistry at Boston University. I believe that my academic success, combined with my extensive volunteer work, provides an excellent background for the rigors of clinical medicine. I am particularly blessed to have a doctor in the family. Through my father, I have seen the demands of being a physician and the commitment that is required to keep abreast of technological advances. I look forward to meeting this challenge and becoming part of such a dynamic field. Until then, I will continue to accompany my dad to the clinic on weekends, to chip away at our inner city health care problem one patient at a time. It is all one person can do.

Our Assessment: The charm of this statement is that it is written in the candidate's own voice. By focusing on her volunteer endeavors, along with the power of her father's example, she crafted an honest and memorable essay that truly highlighted her strengths. The committee was also impressed that the candidate did not focus on her status as an underrepresented minority – although she mentioned it in the third paragraph, she did so in the context of a volunteer experience that meant a lot to her. She made her accomplishments the focus of the statement, rather than her minority status.

Volunteer Experience

On my first day in Haiti, I heard the devastating sounds of a rescue vehicle. The rickety truck, which was the city's only "ambulance," carried a four-year-old earthquake victim to the makeshift public hospital. To my horror, the girl did not survive her injuries, due to the lack of expertise at the facility. In this impoverished village, where nearly every building had collapsed, even simple diagnostic measures were impossible to find.

At 18, I was overwhelmed by the dire conditions in my parents' homeland. Despite their best efforts, they could never have prepared me for the poverty and disease that continue to haunt the nation. Most of the local children - including my extended family members – waited for days to be seen by a doctor. Sadly, in the absence of antibiotics, even curable infections had tragic consequences. For the first time, I understood why my parents had decided to leave Haiti and move to Miami. The abysmal sadness on the island – and the devastating impact of the earthquake - was nearly too much to bear.

When I returned to Miami with my relief team, my desire to help others assumed a new sense of urgency. Before my trip, I was not sure how my intellectual gifts could best serve society. Afterwards, I was determined to make a difference in a country such as Haiti, whose residents did not have access to medical care. With this in mind, I pursued a degree in Toxicology and Public Health at the University of Florida, including the most challenging courses, research projects, and volunteer experiences, to prepare for a career in medicine. For my senior project, I developed a program to promote the use of childhood immunizations in developing nations; my rewarding time in rural India, where we implemented the program, revealed the challenges of serving a disadvantaged population.

To enhance my skills, I enrolled in a Master's program in Epidemiology and Community Health at Johns Hopkins University, which I plan to complete in June of 2012. This challenging experience has opened my mind to the many ways that I can contribute to the health care profession. In the summer of 2010, I worked at the Center for Disease Control in Atlanta, where I published a report about the mortality trends in Central America. I also developed an educational campaign for the use of Gardasil, which is a vaccine that prevents the human papillomavirus that causes cervical cancer.

Whenever possible, I assist physicians who provide primary care to poor and rural communities. In the summer of 2009, I taught classes in disease prevention at a clinic in Haiti. The patients' deep appreciation for our time and commitment was a tremendous source of fulfillment to me. Later, I returned to the island after the devastating earthquake in 2010, which killed thousands of residents and left thousands more with permanent injuries. One day, when the attending physician was ill, I served as the translator between the patients and the physician in the exam room. This experience literally changed my life. During the exams, I observed the difference between clean wounds and infected ones; I also learned how to identify and treat various parasitic infections. Despite our primitive diagnostic techniques, we did our best to provide exemplary care in a compassionate manner. We also taught the children the importance of clean water, hygiene, and safe foods, could reduce the spread of contagious diseases in the aftermath of the earthquake. By doing so, we made a tangible difference in their lives.

After exploring different aspects of health care, I am convinced that I can make the strongest contribution by providing medical care to disadvantaged populations. By honing my skills as a scientist, researcher, and public health advocate, I have cultivated many of the traits I will need to thrive as a physician. As a scientist, I have learned how to evaluate evidence and make intelligent, well-reasoned decisions. As a researcher, I have transformed theoretical findings into promising clinical applications. Through my work in public health, I have tackled the complex challenges of serving vulnerable populations. Most importantly, from building trusting relationships with my patients, I have developed the compassion to assume these challenges with optimism and grace.

Our Assessment: This candidate had an impeccable academic record and considerable experience in public health. In this statement, she focused on her volunteer work in Haiti, which inspired her to enroll in medical school. Her recommendation letters confirmed her maturity and stamina throughout her time on the island.

Volunteer Experience

Somewhere in the middle of my two-month hospitalization for anorexia, I decided that I wanted to become a doctor. My decision would probably have surprised the physicians and nurses on staff, who weren't quite convinced that my recovery would "take." I had, after all, "resisted treatment" in nearly every way possible. Yet the maturation process that marked my recovery somehow showed me that my physician had saved my life, despite my valiant efforts to thwart him. Our initial adversarial relationship eventually morphed into one of mutual respect, which left Dr. Gregory Jennings among my small collection of heroes.

I admire physicians like Dr. Jennings, who understand both what is said and what is held back, and who treat all patients with respect. Eventually, once he had my attention, Dr. Jennings became an impromptu teacher who took the extra time to instruct me in anatomy, the disease process, and personal responsibility. He also convinced me to become a peer counselor at La Hacienda, the treatment program from which I graduated. During my stay there, I gained an appreciation for the personal challenges that patients with anorexia and bulimia face long after their formal treatment ends. Dr. Jennings thought that my perspective as a patient in recovery would be invaluable in the treatment process. I was honored and humbled by his faith in me.

Within six months, I advanced to a paid position as an intake administrator at La Hacienda. The clinic, which provides both inpatient and outpatient services in Fort Worth, caters to a predominantly Spanish-speaking population. My job involves taking histories, performing simple procedures and providing peer counseling. I try to use the knowledge I have gained from my own hospitalization to formulate the right set of questions to ask each patient, but I am constantly reminded of how much I have to learn. When I see a young girl who seems to be the picture of health, I quickly remind myself of the dangerous "hidden behaviors" that she may demonstrate as part of the binge/purge cycle. Likewise, when I record food intakes, I remind myself of my own tendency to exaggerate the content of my meals to please the staff members. Gingerly, knowledgeably, and always with respect, I probe the prospective patient for signs of a potentially life-threatening eating disorder.

One particular patient stole my heart. Angela, a 15-year-old from Honduras, was already a mother of a year-old infant. In a household with seven extended family members, no one questioned her diet until she could no longer produce enough breast milk to feed baby Carlos. Angela's mother drove more than 200 miles to get help at La Hacienda, not knowing how the family would ever be able to pay. Throughout the lengthy intake interview, Carlos played happily at his mother's feet, as she sang the theme song to "Beauty and the Beast." He had no idea that his mother would die just three days later.

Losing Angela convinced me that I can make my best contribution to the medical profession by specializing in the early diagnosis and treatment of eating disorders. Although being a survivor does not give me any special insight into finding a cure, I am painfully aware of the hidden symptoms of the disease, along with the psychological issues that accompany it. I am eager to pursue any (and all) preventive methods, including the potential use of psychotropic drugs.

Throughout the next year, as I complete the admissions process for medical school, I will continue my work at La Hacienda to win my patients' confidence. They are, in every respect, a motley bunch; black, white, straight, gay, college graduates and illiterates. Some choose to enroll, while others are dragged kicking and screaming by their distraught families. Some are in such complete denial that their chances for survival are miniscule. All are my sisters and brothers in this hellacious disease.

Throughout my hospitalization, I wondered if my survival meant that God had a special purpose for me in life. Now, three years after completing the program, I am 100% certain of what that purpose is. By surviving an eating disorder, I have been given the chance to not only share my experience with others, but to be the champion for an eventual cure. The lessons I learned from Dr. Jennings in openness and compassion have shaped my understanding of medicine and will enable me to become the type of doctor I admire.

<u>Our Assessment</u>: Few statements are as raw, honest, and powerful as this one; the candidate truly bared her soul and wrote from the heart. Ultimately, her excellent grades, experience as a counselor, and sterling recommendation letters won the committee over. They knew that she had what it took to become a

compassionate physician.

Volunteer Experiences

Before my step-sister was diagnosed with anorexia, eating disorders were a foreign concept to me. Although I had read the same magazines as other girls my age – and had certainly experienced peer pressure, I was strangely immune to the fixation on diet and exercise.

Sarah's illness was a revelation to me on many levels. Tall, popular, and athletic, she was 18 months older than me and my first peer role model. Compared to my friends, who lacked the benefits of an upscale childhood in the heart of Manhattan, Sarah seemed savvy and sophisticated. When Sarah's mother became concerned about her dramatic weight loss, she asked my dad, who is a veteran pediatrician, to investigate. My father enrolled Sarah in the inpatient program for eating disorders at Milwaukee General Hospital. She died there 42 days later at age 18.

Sarah's death overwhelmed my family and became a milestone event in my life. Devastated by the loss, I felt compelled to understand anorexia better. That quest has ultimately has led me to pursue a career in medicine. The summer after Sarah's death, I volunteered at the Milwaukee General Hospital program for eating disorders, where Sarah was enrolled for the last few weeks of her life. I began as an office worker who fielded phone calls, took messages, and filed charts. I quickly assumed clinical duties, such as preparing medications, weighing patients and distributing juice and snacks. Whenever possible, I listened to the patients lament their lack of control over their bodies during group therapy sessions. The stories I heard, although painful and shocking, deeply touched my heart.

After a particularly emotional session, I asked the clinic's director, Dr. Jane Baker, whether I should continue with the work. She encouraged me to become a peer counselor who would provide the girls with a kind and empathetic ear. After meeting the girls and getting to know them, I couldn't possibly say no. For the past four years, I have spent nearly every weekend and summer volunteering at the clinic, where I have earned the trust of many fine young women who are struggling with this disease. With every new patient, I offer my friendship to someone who is many ways like me: young, talented and seeking a happy future. Yet I am also painfully aware that these patients are victims of a deadly disease with complex psychological origins.

The work is draining. Sometimes, we lose a patient and I will find myself overwhelmed by depression; it is such an unexplainable and senseless death. Nevertheless, I always return for my next shift and my next patient, because I am still needed – and I truly believe I can make a difference. Sadly, the disease also encourages treachery. Sometimes I think I have helped someone, only to discover that they are bingeing or taking laxatives on the sly. It is painful, but I don't consider it a failure. Instead, I come back every day and just keep trying. Although many girls have called me a "godsend," I don't know for sure whether I have actually saved any lives. But I *do* know that I am committed and motivated enough to make this mission my life's work.

During the past two decades, eating disorders have claimed a staggering number of lives. Most victims are successful, attractive young women like Sarah, who have promising futures. Sadly, rather than pursue their goals and fulfill their potential, they become obsessed with an unattainable body image that leads them down a dangerous path to emaciation and death. I simply cannot ignore a problem of such magnitude.

Since Sarah's death, I have committed my life to becoming a physician who specializes in eating disorders. Because the condition is multifaceted in scope, its treatment requires an integrated approach between general practitioners, pediatricians, cardiologists and psychiatrists. Those who specialize in the area, as I plan to do, will pool our resources to save our patients. It is an astonishing challenge, but one I feel called to achieve. It is my legacy to Sarah – and the most important goal in my life.

Our Assessment: This statement is simply written, but extremely powerful. By sharing the story of her step-sister's death and what it meant to her, the candidate revealed her commitment to working with patients who have eating disorders. Her recommendation letters from two physicians at the clinic confirmed her extraordinary communication skills, which are an integral part of clinical medicine.

Volunteer Experience

At age six, Zander knew more about life than I did. He had goals and dreams, with no fear of what the future might hold. Despite his youth and innocence, I found myself looking up to him. I silently prayed that he would beat the cancer that had started to ravage his body.

Zander was the first patient I met when I began my volunteer work at Milwaukee Children's Hospital. At first glance, he looked just like the other patients who were hooked up to machines, yet I immediately sensed something different about him. During our first conversation, Zander told me his dream of becoming a firefighter, an astronaut and a zookeeper. When he asked me what I wanted to do, he was puzzled when I couldn't respond. "Don't you have dreams? Why not?" Before I could offer a plausible explanation, Zander went on to explain that it didn't matter what anyone else thought. "If you want to do it, do it."

Zander's simple words of encouragement taught me more about career planning than any workshop or counselor ever could. Each week, I looked forward to talking with him, particularly when he seemed to become stronger and more confident. Even after he lost his hair to chemotherapy, Zander retained his quick wit and the sparkle in his eyes. I was delighted by his intelligent sophistication.

Finally, I worked up the strength to ask the doctor about Zander's prognosis. Sadly, his body was not responding to the chemotherapy and was slowing shutting down. As Zander began to lose his battle against cancer, he looked sad and helpless in his large hospital bed. After helping me to find my way, it broke my heart to see him so lost and alone. Zander had always been so upbeat and optimistic that I never thought I would lose him. But I did, just one month later.

At the time of Zander's death, I was frustrated because I could not help him get better. Sadly, he never got the chance to make his dreams come true. For several days, I mourned his seemingly "unfulfilled life," until I considered his optimism and persistence. So many people on this earth never have the courage to dream. They are paralyzed by fears and doubts about what will happen if they take a chance and do not get the outcome they expect. Zander's life was a success simply because he *had* dreams, even if they did not come true. Thanks to him, I also had a dream to pursue.

Wherever I go, Zander will be part of my life, giving me the courage to make my dreams a reality. Although I couldn't save him, I realized that there are thousands of kids just like Zander who need my help. As a pediatric oncologist, I can find a cure for cancer and possibly save a child's life. Ambitious? Sure. But Zander wouldn't have it any other way.

Our Assessment: There's an old adage in writing essays: "show them, don't tell them." In this essay, the candidate shows us his maturity, compassion, and motivation through his experience with Zander. The rest of his application revealed the technical details that the committee needed to see, such as his grades, test scores, activities, and recommendation letters. In contrast, this essay gave them a glimpse into the candidate's heart.

Volunteer Experience

When I was ten years old, my beloved aunt lost her hearing unexpectedly. The culprit, a cancerous tumor on her Eustachian tube, became a profound source of fear to me. When I visited my Otolaryngologist for a preventive screening, I asked him a number of questions about this illness, which apparently ran in families. I was saddened to learn that my Aunt Lisa did not need to die at 41; with early diagnosis and treatment, she might have survived her illness. By talking to Dr. Jones about the risks and symptoms of this disease, I gained a new admiration for his ability to preserve her patients' lives. In my heart, I yearned to make a similar difference in my own career.

In the same spirit, I volunteered for the Central American Relief Project, which provides educational and social support to families that have been displaced by civil war in their native countries. At their headquarters in Miami, where thousands of people have sought refuge in the past year, I realized the many blessings that I took for granted, such as food, shelter and medical care. Without these necessities, even the simplest infections became life threatening. For the first time, I understood the importance of what I had to offer the world, on a personal, professional, and spiritual level. I came home each night with a powerful incentive to use my gifts to help others.

In 2008, I fulfilled my parents' life-long dream when I became the first member of our family to attend college. Outside the classroom, I have balanced the demands of a challenging biochemistry curriculum with leadership roles in several campus organizations. During the 2006-2007 academic year, I led Alpha Beta Gamma's fundraising efforts on behalf of cancer research, which raised more than $50,000 for the cause. I also served as the captain of Emory's women's volleyball team, which won third place at the national finals. By honing my skills on and off the court, I have learned the power of focus and optimism in attaining a goal. No matter how my game unfolds, I hold my head high and keep on playing; each shot offers a new chance for hope and victory.

Beyond academia, my most rewarding activity is volunteering at the Cancer Treatment Center of Orlando, where I provide administrative support to their busy staff. Last summer, I also shadowed Dr. Joy Smith, a radiation oncologist who treats patients with metastases. Every shift provided an opportunity to learn more about oncology, including the role of surgery, chemotherapy, and radiation in the treatment of cancer. With honesty and compassion, Dr. Smith helped each patient select the best protocol for his/her specific needs; she also provided a source of comfort and support during a difficult time.

As I watched Dr. Smith, I was impressed by her ability to form positive relationships with people of different ages, backgrounds, and experiences. Every case, whether minor or debilitating, captured 100% of her time and attention. By answering questions and explaining each procedure, she made each patient an equal partner in the healing process. I am grateful for the opportunity to observe Dr. Smith's personalized approach to medicine. Even in challenging situations, she empowers her patients to achieve the best possible outcome.

Last summer, I completed an internship in pediatric oncology, which confirmed my goal of becoming an effective and compassionate physician. I am eager to devote my life to this challenging profession, which will combine my passion for science with my desire to work with people. My long-term goal is to specialize in oncology and use my education to alleviate the suffering of cancer patients. After graduation, I hope to affiliate with a large teaching hospital in the U.S., where I can conduct additional research into tumor growth and metastases. Additionally, I plan to lend my skills to humanitarian groups that serve disadvantaged people, such as the deserving families I met at the Central American Relief Project. By doing so, I can share the benefits of my education with people who would not otherwise receive medical care.

As a child, I was excited to discover God's plan for my life; by opening my heart to different people, places and experiences, I have acknowledged my profound opportunity to make a difference as a physician. If given the chance, I will use my skills to help people like my Aunt Lisa fight their battle against cancer; I will give every patient the absolute best that I have to offer.

Our Assessment: By opening the statement with her aunt's story, this candidate personalized her narrative and made it memorable. It also provided a compelling explanation for her choice of specialty.

Volunteer Experience

The year I turned six, my father lost his leg in a car accident that was caused by a drunk driver. Afterwards, he spent three months at the Tarrytown Rehabilitation Hospital, where I visited him every day. At first, I was frightened by this staid, strange-smelling environment; however, I quickly realized that the place was full of positive energy. Throughout my father's recovery, I accompanied him to his physical therapy sessions, where he learned how to walk with the aid of a prosthetic leg. I couldn't imagine anything more rewarding than being the doctor who had created such a miracle.

When I told my family that I wanted to be a doctor, they thought it was cute. No one realized that I had experienced an epiphany at the rehab facility, which had totally changed my life. Since then, I have devoted the past fifteen years to preparing myself for the challenges of medical school. I am graduating at the top of my class with dual majors in chemistry and biology and have successfully completed independent research in both areas. In addition, I am also completing a pilot study at Rutgers University that examines the effects of mild electrical currents on muscular regeneration and traumatic nerve damage in rats. Although still in its infancy, my research may eventually help paraplegics to walk again. In fact, from working on the project, I am convinced that a cure for paralysis is closer than anyone thinks.

Despite my academic success, I feel most prepared for medicine because of my volunteer work. Since the summer I turned 16, I have volunteered at the Tarrytown Rehabilitation Facility, where my father was a patient many years ago. Although my initial duties were limited to visiting patients and handing out magazines, I quickly advanced to a hands-on role. I was amazed at the number of pre-med volunteers who quickly came and left the facility. "It's too depressing," they would say, to work with patients who had limited hope for recovery. Not me. I continually marvel at the human body's ability to regenerate and repair damaged cells. For most of our patients, they are only as hopeless as they feel.

From my first days at Tarrytown, I was fortunate to have a kind and generous mentor. Amazingly, my supervisor, Dr. Jennings, remembered me from my father's illness more than a decade earlier. I was honored by her invitation to accompany her on her evening rounds, which offered a revealing look at rehabilitative medicine. During my first month, I met Mr. Sanders, who had lost his right leg below the knee in an industrial accident. Initially, he was an angry and bitter man who could not face the failure of his own body. To help Mr. Sanders, we needed to connect with him on numerous levels. At any given session, Dr. Jennings was part doctor, part therapist and part friend. Although she could not fix all of Mr. Sanders' problems, including his familial and financial concerns, she developed a customized care plan that allowed him to eventually walk again.

I was grateful that Mr. Sanders accepted me so quickly. He often mentioned how much I reminded him of his 20-year-old daughter, who had considered becoming a nurse. Because his rehab was difficult, it was not unusual for Mr. Sanders to cry in frustration, which was difficult for me to observe. The pain of his loss, which forced him to see his body differently, was identical to what my father had experienced. With this in mind, I became the diligent cheerleader that Mr. Sanders needed, who relished every milestone of his recovery. My greatest joy was the moment when I saw Mr. Sanders walk with a prosthetic leg for the first time. I got a hard lump in my throat when gave me a bear hug. "I couldn't have done it without you, Sara." For the first time in my life, I felt invaluable to someone. I also knew that I couldn't settle for a career that would offer me anything less.

My only frustration with Mr. Sanders was that I couldn't do more. Since I wasn't a medical doctor, I lacked the ability to fully understand his injury and to plan an effective care plan. My goal is to fill this void by pursuing a career in rehabilitative medicine and spinal cord regeneration. I am particularly encouraged by recent advancements in the field, including novel ways to stimulate damaged nerve cells. In ten years, I plan to be at the forefront of this field, which will allow me to make the recoveries of patients like my dad and Mr. Sanders better, faster and less traumatic. As I realized at age six, there isn't anything more wonderful that I can do with my life.

Our Assessment: This essay is simple, personal, and focused on two aspects of the candidate's life – her father's recovery and her first patient as a volunteer at the rehab center. By limiting her discussion to these topics, she showed a side of herself to the committee that they would not otherwise see.

Volunteer Experience

I first realized the powerful role of a physician when I was rushed into the emergency room of Milwaukee General Hospital. At the time, I was a 16-year-old daredevil who had managed to total my car trying to drive in an ice storm. Fortunately, fate spared me from permanent physical damage, but not from excruciating pain. I broke four bones in my left leg and needed extensive surgery to repair them. I also needed physical therapy to rebuild the damaged tendons.

My two months in rehab were a humbling experience. In a single moment, the quality of my life completely changed. I went from being an independent athlete to a helpless rehab patient who needed help to go to the bathroom. It wasn't easy for me to handle, yet my initial anger was mitigated by the wonderful doctor in Milwaukee who assumed my case. Dr. Gates was a third-year resident who was completing her rotation in rehabilitative therapy. During my first week in the hospital, she developed a care plan for me that was aggressive yet manageable. Her most challenging role was that of counselor. Dr. Gates always encouraged me and kept me moving. As a result, I was blessed to regain the total use of my leg several weeks sooner than expected. Although I never admitted it out loud, I knew in my heart that Dr. Gates was responsible.

The accident sidelined my high school football career and forced me to alter my career plans. Before the crash, I had planned to major in physical education and possibly become a coach. Afterwards, I realized that Dr. Gates was an exceptional coach in her own right, minus the pigskin and whistle. Inspired by her example, I set my sights on a career in medicine.

My experience as the University of Wisconsin has been particularly fulfilling because of my independent research in pain management. Under the direction of Dr. Ralph Lee, I have examined the effects of alternative medical treatments in reducing pain. Dr. Lee's background in Chinese herbs and acupuncture provides a fascinating contrast to the Western modalities of anti-inflammatory drugs and physical therapy. Although my primary interest is in sports and athletic injuries, our treatments have also been successful for patients who suffer from migraines, chronic back problems and post-surgical complications. One patient particularly inspired me.

Brad and I were exactly the same age and shared remarkably similar lifestyles. Before he enrolled in Vanderbilt University, he had also been a star player on his high school football team. Sadly, during Vanderbilt's homecoming game, Brad's pelvis was crushed when he was tackled by two linemen while trying to complete a 50-yard run. As Dr. Lee's patient, Brad experimented with herbs, pain killers, anabolic steroids and acupuncture to control his chronic pain. Nothing helped. After several frustrating weeks, Dr. Lee remembered a rare peppermint-based herbal derivative that was indigenous to his native China. A recent article in the *Lancet* suggested that it might play a role in mitigating pain in post-surgical patients. Dr. Lee felt it was worth a try. He sourced the herb and gave it to Brad as part of an experimental protocol. As I am writing this, I can't explain why it worked..... but it did. As his pain abated, Brad, progressed through his physical therapy, moved to an assisted living facility, and ultimately returned to college. He exceeded everyone's highest expectations.

Because of Brad and Dr. Lee, I am committed to a career in pain management. Due to the slow pace of researching, testing, and new drug approval, Western medicine leaves many patients without a viable way to mitigate pain. As a result, many patients self-medicate or rely on untested materials and questionable guidance. Without an aggressive and informed advocate like Dr. Lee, they miss the opportunity to evaluate experimental treatments. Although "untested" by the FDA, many of these methods work; in fact, some are the ONLY effective relief for Brad and many others who have exhausted the currently approved treatments.

The medical community needs to support these experimental programs and accelerate the drug evaluation and approval process. Ideally, at XXX Medical School, we can co-ordinate our pain research with that of other universities, which will allow us to integrate additional options into our treatment plans. I look forward to following in Dr. Lee's footsteps and pursuing a challenging career in this area. By following his lead, I can help patients like Brad recover faster from their injuries and manage their pain more effectively.

Our Assessment: Initially, this candidate planned to focus on his high school injury and its long-term effect on him. Instead, he used that story as an introduction to a broader statement that discussed his volunteer work with Brad and his interest in pain management. The subsequent statement, although simply written, is highly effective because it links these topics in a logical way. As a result, the reader understands that this is a long-term passion that has grown organically from the candidate's unique experiences.

Volunteer Experience

You never forget the first time you see a dead body. At first glance, the person looks exactly the same as he did in life, yet far more peaceful and still. In my case, the corpse was not a stranger or family member, but a patient I had known at Mercy Hospital. Zachary's calloused hands and dingy clothes revealed his many years in a homeless shelter. However, nobody would guess that Zachary had studied philosophy – or that his only child had died in a boating accident. Sadly, nobody would be able to honor Zachary's memory because he spent the last years of his life doing drugs on the street.

During his many visits to the hospital, Zachary shared several tidbits with me about his colorful life. Every time he was admitted, he promised me that he would stop using drugs, but he never did. One time, I sat with Zachary as the doctor promised him that there was still hope if he would get clean. Sadly, it was a goal unfulfilled. My relationship with Zachary, along with my interactions with his doctors and nurses at the hospital, strengthened my belief that medicine is similar to friendship. Both require loyalty, honesty, an open mind, and being a compassionate listener.

As a child of a psychiatrist, I spent many nights at the dinner table hearing about patients like Zachary. My mother's commitment to the people who relied upon her taught me that being a doctor required far more than prescribing medication. Great doctors formed bonds with their patients and fulfilled their physical and emotional needs. They also possessed an impressive ability to use their knowledge of anatomy and physiology to alleviate suffering. By the time I was a teenager, I was intrigued by every aspect of human health and disease. I wondered if I, too, was destined for a career in medicine.

As a volunteer in the ICU at Mercy Hospital, I began my professional journey. Each afternoon, as I spoke to patients and their families, I was amazed by their wisdom and strength. A 12-year-old boy named Josh told me that he did not talk to his parents about his heart defect because he did not want to make them sad. Instead, Josh accepted his diagnosis and put on a brave front. When I entered his room to play video games, Josh grinned widely, because he knew that I was not there to examine him. I was simply a friend who helped to brighten his day.

Sadly, not every moment was bright and sunny. During my time at Mercy Hospital, I also sat with Josh's parents as they awaited his test results, which provided the answers to difficult questions. On bad days, they collapsed in sadness, unable to fathom Josh's fate. For the first time, I realized that physicians do not simply treat a patient, but an entire family. The responsibilities are enormous, but extremely gratifying.

My mentor, Dr. Lee, told me that good doctors merely treat their patients, while *great* doctors get to know them first. During my internship with him at Our Lady of Fatima Hospital, I had the privilege of working with great doctors. Over the summer, I became a part of the health care team by taking vitals, such as blood pressure, height, and weight. By watching Dr. Lee, I also learned how to earn our patients' trust by treating them with empathy and compassion. Dr. Lee greeted every patient with a handshake and a smile. Regardless of his schedule, he enthusiastically answered their questions and soothed their fears. By the end of the summer, I understood – and appreciated – the many traits that made Dr. Lee a great doctor.

A year later, when I sat with Zachary's lifeless body in the hospital morgue, it changed the way that I thought about medicine. Before his death, I always had a positive outlook about the profession. I knew there was a possibility of death, but I never allowed myself to fully accept it. I also ignored the sad reality that some patients are complicit in their own deaths, even when they are treated by great doctors.

As I embark upon my professional journey, I am more aware of its benefits and drawbacks. Medicine is a lifetime commitment that requires courage, empathy, and a positive mental attitude. To survive the bad times, I must learn from them and use that knowledge to help future patients. In medicine, every day brings the hope of a new treatment or discovery that can save a person's life. It also brings a chance to form new connections and friendships, to ensure that no patient will take that journey alone.

Our Assessment: This is a remarkable statement from a remarkable candidate. By framing his volunteer experiences through his relationship with Zachary, he allowed the reader to accompany him on a sad and emotional journey. His insight about the limitations of medicine, although poignant, differentiated him from other candidates.

Chapter 3: Inspired by an Issue or Cause

Many candidates use the personal statement to discuss an issue, cause, or personal experience that confirmed their desire to pursue a medical career. For the essay to be compelling, the issue must be something that you not only think about, but have taken the time to work on. For example, everyone (theoretically) opposes drunk driving, but few join advocacy groups such as Students Against Drunk Driving. Likewise, many people talk about the importance of health education, but few participate in programs to promote HIV/AIDS awareness. Ideally, in your personal statement, you should express more than passive idealism; instead, you should discuss a problem that you cared enough to *solve*.

Second, do not ignore the most important aspect of the statement, which is to explain *why* this issue or experience is important to you. If you (or someone you know) suffered a loss because of an issue, how did it affect you – and how did you overcome that setback? What have you done since then to prevent similar obstacles in the future? If written honestly and intelligently, your statement can reveal a level of depth and insight that the committee would never learn about any other way.

A common sense caveat, however: if you choose to discuss a difficult experience, be sure to explain how you have learned and grown from it as a person. Your goal is not to elicit sympathy, but to position yourself as a survivor who has much to offer whatever medical school accepts you.

Here are several successful answers to this question from candidates who were admitted to medical school. By design, we have grouped the essays in the following sub-categories:

Commitment to Public Health
Commitment to Advocacy
Passion for Research

To protect the privacy of the writer, the names of all people, classes, schools, places, teams, activities, and companies have been changed.

Commitment to Public Health

When I picked up the phone, I could barely hear my brother's voice. "Father is dead," he cried. "Please come home." As I rushed to the airport, I could not understand why our father had succumbed to a simple case of the flu. By the time I arrived at the hospital, I learned that he had actually died of congestive heart failure, which had been diagnosed two years earlier. As a Cuban immigrant, my father fell through the cracks of the U.S. health care system. Unable to afford insurance or treatment, he suffered in silence until that fateful night, when he died on the way to the hospital.

In the Miami neighborhood where I was born and raised, the disparity of health care between wealthy citizens and poor minorities was impossible to ignore. For most of my family and friends, even the cost of immunizations was well beyond our reach. My father's death at 36 forced me to take a closer look at the availability of medical care in America. I was astonished by what I learned. Every day, in every U.S. city, people die from treatable illnesses because they do not have health insurance. As the son of such a victim, I am committed to doing my part to prevent these unnecessary deaths.

To this end, I have dedicated my career to identifying and resolving the complex political, social, and economic barriers to health care. After completing my undergraduate degree in public health, I helped to design and implement a pilot program on behalf of Miami Dade Behavioral Health Services to identify and treat patients with mental illness. To ensure participation in the Cuban-American community, in which mental illness is considered taboo, I developed an educational program about the underlying diseases and their treatments. With the assistance of various support groups, counselors, nurses, and psychiatrists, I provided support and treatment for those who had been ostracized by their community.

Later, the Mental Health Association of Florida asked me to expand the pilot program to serve a particularly troubling population - homeless people with multiple complications, including a long history of psychiatric hospitalizations, incarcerations, and physical disabilities. We offered an array of services for our clients, including outreach, prevention, healthcare, and assistance with housing, employment, and substance abuse. The program delivered impressive results; in the first year, we reduced our clients' number of homeless days, jail time, and psychiatric hospitalizations by 75%.

In honor of my father, I also support the work of Florida Seniors United (FSU), which provides health care to seniors who suffer from chronic conditions such as diabetes, hypertension, arthritis, and congestive heart failure. By combining regular health assessments with a comprehensive health care plan, FSU enables many seniors to obtain affordable care while living in their own homes. Eventually, I hope to design a health plan for the elderly that uses electronic medical records, which can reduce the number of duplicate tests, adverse drug reactions, and unnecessary hospitalizations.

As a graduate student in Public Health at the University of Florida, I am researching the most practical and efficient ways to deliver care to underserved populations. First, I am drafting a policy proposal to expand the coverage of Medicare Part B and eliminate the "donut hole" that denies benefits to seniors who were born in specific years. Second, I have joined a team of physicians and pharmacists to develop a population-based software system that will allow us to develop predictive models for all types of financial, administrative, and care management applications. Eventually, we can use the system to manage risk by evaluating access to care, predicting high-risk users, improving quality, monitoring outcomes, analyzing reimbursements, and improving accuracy in underwriting.

Because of what I have witnessed, as both a Cuban-American immigrant and an advocate for public health, I am deeply motivated to improve and transform American's health care system. Within my lifetime, I hope to champion a fair and equitable system that offers quality medical care for all people, regardless of their race, location, or socioeconomic status. To some, my goal is impossible; to others, it is an admirable dream. To me, it is a lifelong quest to answer questions that others are too timid to ask. In a country as wealthy as the United States, no one should die from a treatable illness the way my father did. As long as I draw breath, I will fight the barriers that prevented him from receiving the care he needed to enjoy a long and healthy life.

Our Assessment: This emotional and persuasive statement was written by a candidate with more than a decade of experience in public health. By opening the essay with the story about his father's death, he personalized the narrative and immediately gained the reader's interest. Nevertheless, this essay was also risky, because it did not "sell" his academic and clinical skills, which are important aspects of the selection process. Thankfully, the author's recommendation letters documented his accomplishments in these areas, which were quite impressive. His application was well received.

Commitment to Public Health

At age 16, I heard Magic Johnson speak at the International AIDS conference in London. Afterwards, I became perplexed by this epidemic's unmet cry for help. Why, I wondered, did it take an infected basketball star to convince people that AIDS was a global health crisis? Wasn't it enough that millions of people in South Africa had already succumbed to this deadly virus? Mr. Johnson's speech illuminated the accomplishments of the dedicated researchers who are working tirelessly to stop the spread of HIV. Ultimately, his work as an advocate sparked my desire to specialize in global health. By concentrating in infectious diseases, I will use my international expertise to address the most pressing health issues in the developing world.

As a child in Beijing, I witnessed the challenges faced by a developing nation, including poverty, hunger, disease, and the consequences of political instability and rapid urbanization. The sight of impoverished children begging for food on the polluted streets left a lasting impression on me. When my brother contracted Dengue fever, I was too young to look beyond his symptoms. In retrospect, I realize that my brother had contracted an infectious disease that continues to have deleterious implications in developing parts of the world. When I returned to California, I recognized the vast disparities between developing and industrialized nations. For example, infectious diseases that are treatable in North America, such as tuberculosis, continue to kill millions of people in disadvantaged parts of the world. As a citizen of a wealthy nation, I am determined to improve the quality of life for people who do not enjoy similar benefits.

At Stanford University, I completed a dual degree in political science and public health. By evaluating the social, economic, and political influences in different societies, I realized that many of the underlying factors that guide public health are the result of government policy. For my senior research project, I spent a semester researching, analyzing and critiquing American policy towards malaria in the developing world. By doing so, I gained a profound understanding of the obstacles that governments face to combat the pandemic spread of infectious diseases, including the lack of education, the transmittance of information across cultural boundaries, drug resistance, the need for sustainability, and the complex relationships among organizations and nations. With an MD/MPH, I can develop cost-effective strategies for disease prevention and health care promotion, which will permit me to tackle the most challenging health issues.

As a volunteer for the International AIDS Relief organization, I have devoted the past three summers to a public health facility in Ghana that serves the needs of local residents. The experience has literally changed my life. During our exams and intake interviews, I discovered that few patients had a clear understanding of how the disease was transmitted – or the preventive measures they should take in their everyday behavior. Even worse, the stigma of the disease and the proliferation of poor and misleading information made it difficult to attract students to our free educational classes about HIV. On a short-term basis, we did our best to distribute condoms and provide basic health care serves. Sadly, in the absence of reliable infrastructure and sustainable global health programs, few people in Ghana will ever enjoy the level of care that they deserve. Ultimately, it is their plight that motivates my application to the MD/MPH program at XXXXX.

In many developing nations, including Ghana, preventive care is virtually nonexistent. As a result, health care providers have a wealth of opportunities to make a lasting difference in the communities they visit. Even simple measures, such boiling water and washing hands, can reduce the spread of communicable diseases. On a practical basis, these programs require time, money, and dedication to implement. By becoming a physician and public health advocate, I hope to play an integral part in this process.

If admitted, I will bring several strengths to your program. As the daughter of a U.S. diplomat, I have been privileged to live in disparate parts of Asia, Europe, the Middle East, and America. By continually adapting to different places, I have become fluent in French, Spanish, Russian, and Mandarin. Additionally, by mentoring Cuban and Haitian refugees, I have used my communication skills to help children adapt to a foreign culture. These skills will also enable me to establish essential relationships with people who share my goal of improving the quality of health in underserved communities.

Inspired by Magic Johnson, I am committed to pursuing a dual MD/MPH, with a concentration in Infectious Diseases. The constant challenges in this field, along with the rapid pace of medical developments, provide the perfect context for me to pursue my passions. Ideally, by contributing to the unique health initiatives at XXXXX, I can impact the health of patients like Magic Johnson in a positive and meaningful way.

Our Assessment: This candidate had an extraordinary background in public health and international epidemiology, which was the primary topic of her personal statement. Her recommendation letters provided additional details about her commitment to this area, which was a perfect match for the MD/MPH program that she eventually chose.

Commitment to Public Health

Throughout my lifetime, I have overcome tremendous obstacles to become an advocate for health care in my native Namibia. In the remote village where I was raised, there was minimal funding for education. As a result, few children completed primary and secondary school. Fortunately, I was blessed with supportive parents and the tenacity to succeed. After years of struggle, I arrived at the University of Namibia in 1997 to start an undergraduate course in medicine. After five years of mental and physical torture, I graduated with a Bachelor of Medicine and Bachelor of Surgery in 2002. After completing an internship at a provincial hospital, I registered as a medical officer and worked in a busy maternity unit for two years.

In 2004, I was recruited into the Namibian Army and deployed as the medical officer in charge of a battalion of soldiers. My stint in the Army was the most exciting period in my life. As the first Namibian doctor to be trained as a paratrooper, I undertook numerous night missions with American soldiers during military exercises. After a three-year stint in the military medical service, I joined the Department of Obstetrics and Gynecology at the University of Namibia for a Master's degree in obstetrics and gynecology. After graduating in 2009, I joined the regional military hospital as a gynecologist. I worked in this capacity until 2011, when I started a private consulting office for reproductive health matters in Namibia.

After 10 years as a practicing Obstetrician and Gynecologist, I have identified an acute need for research, education and public support for numerous reproductive health issues. Accordingly, I plan to specialize in public health with a bias to maternal and child health. Reproductive care consumes a huge portion of Namibia's health budget, yet the preventive aspects have been neglected in favor of curative medicine. The most pressing issues in Namibia include drug abuse, contraceptive use, sexually transmitted diseases (including HIV-AIDS) and the outcome (and effects) of early pregnancies. My goal is to develop a comprehensive preventive reproductive health plan that educates children, teenagers and young adults about the effects of teenage sexual activity upon their health and longevity.

To achieve a long-term community impact, I will assume a role at the government level to formulate appropriate public health policies and to deliver reproductive health services. The non-governmental organizations that currently provide community-based healthcare in Namibia lack professional support. Working with them on a grassroots level, I will develop and conduct workshops that convey technical knowledge and new developments about reproductive health issues. I will serve as a conduit between the district administrators and the members of the medical fraternity to develop the workshops, train the facilitators and re-train current medical personnel.

To achieve lasting success, Namibia must make immediate improvements in the curricula for doctors, nurses and public health technicians. I will coordinate the university departments that train healthcare providers to emphasize the importance of preventive reproductive care. Further, through research, we will identify better ways to educate our youth about their sexuality and to prevent disease and unwanted pregnancies. With a medical degree from the United States, I will have the tools I need to make a lasting contribution to the health of my nation. Afterwards, I will share my success with future generations of Namibians, who will enjoy better health and increased longevity via informed reproductive choices.

<u>Our Assessment</u>: This candidate had a fascinating background, including a medical degree from a foreign school, military experience as a paratrooper, and a demonstrated commitment to public health initiatives in his native country. In this statement, he explains his goals in a concise and persuasive manner. The candidate was a perfect fit for the program he chose, which specialized in public health education.

Commitment to Public Health

The Body: As I trudged through the sludge-filled Blind River, my stomach churned from the stench of dead and decaying animals. Despite my recent marathon training, I was pushed to my limits by the grueling conditions in rural Louisiana. My passion for adventure inspired me to participate in this project along the contaminated river, which was twenty miles from the nearest city. However, during the intensely challenging conditions in this bug-infested terrain, I concentrated on the goal of my work: to conduct environmental sampling to determine if the toxins from an abandoned factory were responsible for the dramatic increase of rare cancers among the local residents. Despite our difference in age and background, I related to the villagers' concerns regarding the carcinogens. Having lost a loved one to cancer, I empathized with their grief and fear.

The Mind: My father's death from cancer when I was ten taught me a harsh lesson regarding the value of education. Without a college degree, my mother could not find employment that paid more than minimum wage. Starting at age twelve, I helped to support our household by delivering newspapers, washing dishes at a restaurant, and exercising animals at a local farm. I rigorously pursued academic excellence as a way to avoid the hardships that my mother had endured. I became particularly interested in public health, due to the nature of my father's illness. At 22, he was exposed to Agent Orange in the Vietnamese village where his Army unit had served. Fifteen years later, only three members of my father's unit are still alive, due to this deadly carcinogen. His prolonged illness, which devastated our entire family, taught me that I should never take safety for granted; instead, I must ask difficult questions about everything in my environment.

The Community: As an adult, I continue to value the warmth and support in the close-knit town where I was raised. At the same time, I also enjoy traveling from town to town as a public health investigator. Every community I visit provides a new opportunity to increase public awareness regarding health and environmental issues. Over the years, I have received deep satisfaction from the "human" aspects of my research, rather than the scientific details. By listening to the residents of Louisiana, I learned about the conditions at the abandoned factory and I cultivated the friendship and trust of the people in the community. Recently, I brought the students in my Environmental Health class on a "toxic tour" of several disadvantaged neighborhoods in Philadelphia, to increase their awareness of environmental health problems. My goal was to show real-life examples of class topics in our own community and to encourage my students to lobby for improvements on a local level.

The Future: Through research, travel and family experiences, I have observed several crises in public health that require immediate intervention. In some cases, such as the contamination in Louisiana, legal action will be required to remove the toxic waste and restore healthy living conditions. Other cases simply require the development and implementation of a solid educational program throughout the nation. My passion to solve these problems has reinforced my long-term aspiration to work as an advocate for public health. In my heart, I know that my calling is to infuse the nation with a much-needed sense of balance in making decisions that affect the environment and health. Since early childhood, I have invested my energy in promoting these causes in every aspect of my life. Medical school is the next step on my exhilarating educational journey.

Our Assessment: This author used sub-headings to group her topics in a logical way. The breadth of her experiences, which confirmed her interest in public health, set her apart from other candidates with similar goals.

Commitment to Public Health in a Developing Nation

By becoming a physician, I hope to make a lasting contribution to the Arab nation where I was born and raised, where my extended family continues to live. The continuous economic growth in Yemen, which has been fueled primarily by the oil industry, has made a great improvement in the nation's standard of living. However, Yemen's health care system continues to remain substandard and unreliable. Despite a population of nearly one million people, Yemen only has a handful of small hospitals. Few of them receive funding from the federal government, which limits the technological advancements they can offer their patients. There is also a dire lack of training, licensing, and regulations for the health care professionals who are responsible for treating and diagnosing a wide range of illnesses and injuries. As a result, thousands of patients die in Yemen every day because of improper medical care.

An additional complication is the misplaced priorities in health care. In Yemen, the system is governed by money, rather than ethics. Regardless of the severity of the case, patients who have money are always treated first. Those who are indigent are unlikely to be treated at all. In April of 2011, my two cousins got into an auto accident while visiting our extended family in Yemen. Abdul's foot was severely crushed, which required immediate medical treatment. Lee rushed him to the nearest hospital, where she hoped that Abdul would receive proper care and compassion. Sadly, the doctors refused to treat Abdul until the hospital received $5,000 USD. To obtain this amount of money, Lee had to leave Abdul alone at the hospital for several hours while he waited for treatment. If she had not returned with the required fee, Abdul would likely have died in the waiting room.

Ironically, wealthy and insured patients also struggle to obtain quality care. Last winter, my grandfather was hospitalized in Yemen with severe abdominal pain. The facility that admitted him had the highest standards of care in the nation. During the first week, my grandfather's doctors prescribed medication for irritable bowel syndrome, which they insisted was the source of his pain. Unfortunately, his condition continued to deteriorate. Nevertheless, the doctors sent my grandfather home with a stronger medication and told him to "have faith" in their diagnostic skills. The cost for his hospital stay, in which his condition only got worse, was $30,000 USD. A week later, when he returned to the U.S., my grandfather sought treatment for the same symptoms at a public hospital in New York City. Within a day, the doctors determined that he had a carcinoid tumor in his colon, which was the source of his discomfort. My grandfather's condition improved greatly after its removal. Sadly, his case, which is far from unique, reveals the poor training and unethical practices of health care professionals in Yemen.

Because of the high cost and unreliable reputations of many doctors, the people in Yemen often buy their medication directly from the pharmacy, where all drugs are available without a prescription. Sadly, the pharmaceutical industry is not well regulated in Yemen, which makes this approach inherently risky. Although the law requires that all pharmacies have a government license, many owners obtain them by bribing local officials or falsifying their application documents. Then, these unqualified owners engage in deceptive practices to increase their profits, such as diluting the drugs and changing the expiration date in order to sell old medication. There is also a knowledge gap, which prevents the average citizen from choosing the correct drug and dosage for their particular illness. As a result, people often exacerbate their problem by choosing the wrong drug, taking it incorrectly, and ignoring potentially deadly side effects and drug interactions.

Although the public is well aware of these issues, the federal government continues to ignore them. If they invested money in the health care system and enforced strict regulations on the standards for care, medication, and the training of health care professionals, considerable pain, suffering, and loss could easily be prevented. By becoming a physician and building my practice in Yemen, I hope to shed light on these issues and do my part to create an ethical and compassionate solution.

Our Assessment: This is a serious, well written, and well documented statement about an important issue in the author's native country. Because she was applying to a highly competitive program with a focus on international medicine, it was also a highly relevant (and somewhat unusual) topic for the admissions committee. By adding the personal anecdotes about her cousins and grandfather, the candidate gave this essay the detail it needed to be persuasive and memorable.

Commitment to Advocacy for Women

As Anna waited in our office, I marveled at how much she looked like me; we were both short, with dark brown hair and a lithe, athletic build. Yet upon closer scrutiny, our similarities were purely physical. The previous night, while I studied for my psych exam, Anna had been beaten by her abusive husband and was forced to flee with her young child. According to police reports, she had been victimized by her spouse for more than five years, yet she always drifted back to him. At 23, with no education or job skills, Anna couldn't envision any hope of a better future.

For many college students, women like Anna are a sad mystery. In a country with unlimited resources, how could a healthy and smart young woman wind up in such a dismal situation? In my work as a volunteer with Women & Children First, I have learned all too well that Anna's situation is far from unique. Across the globe, women who live in poverty are often victims of physical and emotional abuse. In western nations, they fall prey to abusive boyfriends and husbands who control their behavior and destroy their self-esteem. Even more frightening, many girls in Third World nations are sold into the sex trade, in which they must earn a living by selling their bodies. Without emotional and financial assistance, these women are unable to escape the desperation of their dead-end lives.

As a successful college student, I am blessed with the prospect of a bright future, yet I am painfully aware that I could easily have fallen victim to the same violence as Anna. As a young child, I also struggled with the effects of poverty and sexual abuse. Fortunately, with the help of a qualified therapist, I recovered from this trauma and learned how to build a better life. As a survivor, I am determined to use my skills to provide a voice for others who struggle with the same issues.

Looking back, my traumatic childhood was the catalyst that sparked my passion for learning. At an early age, I began to challenge the limits of my abilities. Despite our meager financial resources, my mother encouraged me to envision a world without boundaries, in which the word "can't" does not exist. As a result, I pursued my education with a vengeance and took the most demanding courses possible. With my eye on a medical career, I chose to major in psychology, to better understand why people do the things they do. In 2010, I will complete my degree in Psychology at Syracuse University, where my student research has focused on memory and eyewitness testimony.

Throughout my undergraduate years, I have been a passionate advocate for the rights of women and children. As a volunteer for Women & Children First, I have been a counselor, mentor, teacher and fundraiser for families in need. I also work for Beloved Lioness, which champions the rights of oppressed women in Third World countries. Since 2009, I have volunteered at a shelter for poor refugees who had fled from violence in their native countries. Some have lost their husbands in civil wars, while others have endured physical and sexual exploitation. All are desperate to remain in the United States, which provides equal rights and freedom to women.

Using my training in psychology, I counsel our clients and help our attorneys translate their testimony between English and Arabic. As a woman who shares their ethnic background, I am a comforting face to many of our female clients, who are hesitant to discuss being molested, raped or sold into prostitution. Their heartbreaking stories opened my eyes to the powerful ways that a compassionate physician can change someone's life. My greatest frustration is that we cannot help everyone; with limited resources, many injustices are simply beyond our reach.

Despite the overwhelming work load, I am energized by the chance to provide physical and emotional care to poor and immigrant patients, who would not otherwise be served. As a United States citizen, I am deeply appreciative of the benefits the country has to offer, including a free society, quality medical care and a fair and just legal system. Yet, as a volunteer, I know that many people do not receive the care they need because of financial and educational limitations. As a physician, I will treat indigent clients like Anna, who desperately need my help. In my quest to protect innocent victims from unspeakable violence, I will never give up.

Our Assessment: This is a strong statement from a woman who is committed to serving as an advocate for oppressed and abused women. In this eloquent statement, she states her case clearly and passionately; her multicultural background was particularly well perceived in the admissions process.

Commitment to Advocacy for Women

As a child in the 1970's, I was mesmerized by the huge social shift in the United States. For the first time, women went to college in record numbers and assumed professional roles that were previously unavailable to them. The development of reliable birth control and the sexual revolution gave us freedoms that my mother and grandmother had never imagined. I was an inquisitive child of the times. With so many available "flavors," I was eager to taste them all.

After completing my BA in Social Work at Vassar College, I accepted a job with Planned Parenthood of Pittsburgh, where we offer a full range of women's health services, including low-cost gynecological exams, pregnancy testing, birth control counseling and programs to prevent and treat sexually transmitted diseases. I also developed a sex education curriculum that promoted contraception, AIDS awareness and sexual abuse prevention. For many years, our services were heralded in the community and we felt safe when we arrived at work. Things would soon change..... for the worse.

In the late 1990's, as the tide shifted regarding women's rights, we became the target of religious and right-wing attacks. For many years, we were the only facility in Beaver County that provided first trimester pregnancy terminations. Unfortunately, a small group of conservatives resented our commitment to performing services that they personally opposed. Soon, protestors began to picket the clinic, accost our patients with propaganda, and threaten their lives. Many days, they blocked the entrances to our building, which made it difficult for patients to come and go. We frequently received bomb threats and had our windows broken by demonstrators. Despite my fears, I felt compelled to take a stand against this intimidation.

I volunteered for a Democratic congressional campaign, where I briefed the candidate on abortion rights and sexuality issues in health care reform. I used my position at Planned Parenthood to lobby at the state level against parental notification laws for minors who received abortions. I also promoted the legalization of RU-486 and pending legislation that would make violent acts committed by clinic protestors part of the proposed "hate crime" bill.

After the congressman's election, I assumed the presidency of the newly-created Pennsylvania Women's Health Advocacy Group in Harrisburg. With the help of a lobbyist, we have coordinated a strategy to promote women's health issues on the state level. In my current position, I research legislation, design lobbying strategies and serve as the liaison with affiliated organizations throughout the state regarding pending policies and bills. Although I am passionate about my work, I have also reached a troubling conclusion – that we are losing the fight against right wing zealots who are committed to reversing Roe V. Wade.

In the past ten years, the federal government has restricted funding to clinics that provide abortion services, which has shuttered facilities in more than a dozen states. Additionally, physicians who perform abortions are choosing to leave the field in record numbers, due to the ongoing threats on their lives. As a result, millions of women must travel long distances to receive the services they need; some cannot find treatment at any price, due to their state's position on Roe v. Wade. Looking ahead, I am determined to fill this void to ensure that all women have equal access to the reproductive services to which they are legally and morally entitled.

Throughout the debate on abortion and birth control, I have been haunted by a sad truth; reversing Roe V. Wade will not stop abortions; it will simply criminalize them and make them more expensive to obtain. On a practical basis, wealthy women will always have access to the services they need, while the poorest women who are least able to raise an unplanned child will be forced into the back alleys where the quality of care is nebulous. My fervent goal is to give all women equal access to family planning services, regardless of their race, location, and socio economic standing. Ironically, after a decade in public service, I have recognized that I can best accomplish this goal by changing professions and becoming a physician who specializes in women's health.

Ironically, as a child in the 70's, I viewed the availability of birth control as a basic right that could never be denied. Since then, I have recognized that it is a privilege that we could easily lose unless we fight vigilantly for it. My motivation to become a doctor is to lead this fight and to ensure the survival of women's rights for future generations. It is a legacy that I will be honored to claim.

This author had a long and illustrious career as an advocate for various feminist causes in Pennsylvania, which this statement covered in a few short paragraphs. Although the statement is somewhat dry, it conveys the candidate's commitment to the cause and her future intentions in an eloquent way.

Committed to Advocacy - HIV/AIDS Awareness

During my freshman year in high school, I learned that my favorite teacher, Mr. Phillips, had contracted HIV from an emergency appendectomy ten years earlier. Although he survived the surgery, the tainted blood that he received made his prognosis anything but rosy.

Mr. Phillips was my inspiration from the moment we met. He was the young, committed role model that a fatherless boy dreams of meeting during his formative years. Regardless of his schedule, Mr. Phillips listened to his students and offered an optimistic view of our everyday problems. I was inspired by his interest in my life, which genuinely made a difference. Accordingly, after high school, I already had my future mapped out: I wanted to become a teacher and coach just like him.

The last few months of Mr. Phillips' tenure were puzzling for me as I witnessed his inexplicable decline. Although he continued to coach our basketball team, Mr. Phillips seemed detached from the activities that had previously engrossed him. Even his appearance changed. At first, I thought that Mr. Phillips was having personal problems or maybe the flu. I was devastated by the announcement of his illness and shattered by the thought of losing such a valued friend.

A few days after Mr. Phillips left our school, I volunteered for a new program to promote AIDS awareness in the community. The Warren Community AIDS Committee began with 15 members, ranging in age from 55 to 14 (me). As the only "young" person in the group, I became our liaison with the local high school, where we planned to have our first seminar. Because of Mr. Phillips, our students already knew that AIDS was a killer; we also feared that we might become its next victim. My first job was to recruit volunteers to deliver informational seminars at the junior high school. Thirty of us went through five days of rigorous training to become AIDS awareness counselors. Through this program, we learned about the causes and transmission of AIDS, teen pregnancy, and STDs, which could be dramatically reduced by condom use. We also learned how to present the material in an effective and responsible manner.

Our first classes were difficult and somewhat amusing. When we presented our material to a seventh-grade health class, it took some time before I could say terms like "vaginal secretions," "ejaculation" and "testicular" without turning beet red. But the message was so powerful and important that I never lost my focus. By the final hour of the program, I knew that the audience was listening. The kids started to open up to us and ask relevant questions about being ready for sex and how to say no. We discussed self-esteem, putting your own safety first, and being true to your own values. We provided the very lectures that I wish someone had given me at the same age.

I continued my work in AIDS awareness throughout college. Because my university is just 30 miles from Warren, I have been able to expand the local pilot program to the campus level. During the past four years, I have trained more than 200 new volunteers to teach AIDS awareness, but we don't limit our presentations to high schools. Instead, we bring our program to any place that will have us, including prisons, women's shelters, hospitals, shopping malls and dorm rooms. We won an award this year from the CDC for having the best university-based AIDS education program in the nation. Most importantly, through this work, I have discovered that preventing HIV is my calling.

When I envision my professional future, I see myself as a primary care physician who treats AIDS patients and their families. It is a cause that deeply touches my soul. My high school teacher, Mr. Phillips, died from AIDS last year, after a long and valiant struggle. I would like to think that if I had been an MD, I could have helped him. I know that he would want me to help others. In my heart, I can't imagine a greater success, or a greater calling, than that.

This statement, although simply written, is honest, heartfelt, and powerful. Initially, the candidate struggled to tell this story, because it was very emotional for him. After careful consideration, he decided to omit most of the details about the AIDS Committee, which one of his recommendation letters would also cover. Instead, he focused exclusively on his motivation to join the group, which eventually guided his career choice. It was a risk that definitely paid off.

Passion for Biotechnology

Knowing my passion for crime novels, my parents assumed that my medical school aspirations were based on my desire to work in forensics. Unbeknownst to them, I entered my university studies with more of an inclination towards biotechnology. Although bacteria, viruses and parasites were fun to learn about, as a college freshman, I was actually more intrigued by cloned sheep and test tube babies. Now in my graduating year, biotechnology remains my principle field of interest.

Twenty years ago, the idea of selling human embryos in an "underground" market was the stuff of James Bond novels, yet the possibility is no longer science fiction. Even nations that support stem cell research, such as China, have seen the development of such a market, which has created a conflict of interest between the urban facilities and rural clinics that supply human embryos. These conflicts have already halted most stem cell research in the United States, and have pushed the commercialization of the underlying technologies overseas. My motivation to attend medical school is to acquire the skills I will need to conduct this cutting-edge research, which will affect not only the future of science but the quality and extension of human life.

My interest in biotechnology was piqued in high school, when I wrote my senior thesis on the bioethics of reproductive technologies. In my subsequent years at the University of London, the topic has grown in controversy with the explosion of stem cell research. My studies in microbiology and immunology have given me the flexibility to learn about diseases, germs, and their applications in biotechnology while simultaneously exploring other fields that allow me to view my scientific knowledge within a global context.

As a college freshman, I got my first taste of the global impact of biotechnology at the University's summit on genomics and biotechnology. Last year, I was a member of a pioneer group that established the school's first student-run bioethics conference. Despite the amazing possibilities and implications, I discovered that few people seemed to possess adequate knowledge about the booming biotechnology industry. From my perspective, there is a compelling need to take this knowledge to the general public to initiate a dialogue about the underlying moral and ethical issues.

After the success of the first bioethics conference, we decided to improve and expand the event for 2008. As this year's co-chair, I am fulfilling our vision of an international conference, which is attracting delegates and speakers from South Korea, India, the Philippines and the United States. Our participants are not just scientists, but internationally recognized experts in medicine, law, business, philosophy, sociology and religion, who will evaluate the issues from a 360-degree angle in diverse academic, social and cultural contexts. By widening the demographics of the conference, we hope to increase awareness and stimulate debate of not only the controversial "hot topics," such as stem cell research, but of lesser discussed (but equally fascinating) issues such as organ transplants, aging, and various forms of life enhancement and extension.

The intense competition in this technologically-driven society has created an unprecedented need for ethical researchers who are motivated by the love of science, rather than profit. In the global village, nations such as China, South Korea, the UK and the US are competing to maintain their positions as world leaders on the frontiers of biotechnological research and development. With my multicultural background, I will be well positioned to satisfy the demand for medical professionals who can bridge the gap between disparate cultures. At XXXXX Medical School, I will acquire the expertise that will enable me to contribute to the ongoing scientific progress in the burgeoning biotechnology industry.

Our Assessment: In this short (but focused) statement, this candidate explains her passion for biotechnology, which is a field in which she has published several papers. Combined with her recommendations from several distinguished researchers who supervised her work, it set her apart from other candidates who were applying for a competitive PhD/MD program.

Passion for Research

"People with vibrant personalities do NOT work in research laboratories." Six years later, my sister's assessment of my introverted personality continues to make me wince.

When I selected a college, I heeded my sibling's concerns about spending too much time in a research lab. Rather than choose a small technical school, I accepted an offer from Yale University, which would allow me to become part of an amazingly diverse population. In this heterogeneous group, I could not only explore my interest in science, but gain a realistic perspective of the role of technology in everyday life. My classes in history and government gave me fascinating insight into the role of medicine in society – and the divergent thoughts about controversial issues such as abortion, euthanasia, and stem cell use. At the same time, my classes in psychology and women's studies revealed the dire need for gender equality in medicine, including the need for additional research into the causes and prevention of breast and ovarian cancers.

Nevertheless, my greatest joy of my educational experience was completing my science classes and preparing for the rigors of medical school. I first became interested in research when I accepted a position in the Department of Neurosurgery at Rhode Island Hospital. After a short training period, I worked independently on a research project to evaluate the efficacy of various surgical techniques on rats. During my second week, I observed my mentor, Dr. John Scott, perform a comparable procedure on a 30-year-old patient with a brain tumor. After the initial shock of seeing an exposed brain, I thought about the connections between this clinical application and my own research. Although my original objective was to gain a better understanding of tumors, my ultimate goal was to save the people I saw on the operating table. With this in mind, I completed the short-term objectives of my projects with renewed vigor. The resulting paper has been submitted to *Neurosurgery* for publication.

This summer, as a participant in Brown University's Summer Undergraduate Research Program, I am learning even more about research and clinical medicine. In my work, I am determining the effect of XXX on induced tumorigenesis. For this particular project, I have assumed responsibility for all aspects of data collection and analysis, which required the mastery of statistical design software. By conducting molecular oncology research for another summer, I have greatly expanded my knowledge and interest in the field. In the case of cancer, research is the only way to overcome the limitations of current clinical treatments.

In addition to my work in the laboratory, I have also explored the clinical side of medicine by volunteering in the Emergency Room of the Bristol County Medical Center during my sophomore year. I was immediately impressed by the staff's sensitivity and compassion. Besides assisting the nurses, I took every opportunity to comfort patients who felt scared and vulnerable. During that same year, I also worked as a live-in companion for a woman who had been severely injured in a car accident. At first, our progress seemed negligible, because each achievement came slowly and painfully. Nevertheless, by the end of the semester, Grace was able to walk with a cane and speak in simple sentences. I was thrilled to be part of her hard-won recovery.

Sadly, despite my sister's admonitions, I must confess that I am still a hopeless "science nerd." However, throughout my years at Yale, I have learned some of my greatest lessons outside of lecture halls and libraries. In the research lab, I have refined my intellectual curiosity and scientific thought processes through a series of progressive challenges. At the hospital, I have developed my interpersonal skills and a greater understanding of others by interacting with a diverse group of people. Finally, in my work with Grace, I have learned that a compassionate caregiver can make the difference between a fearful patient and one who is hopeful and confident. Through it all, I have learned to treasure the simple pleasures of helping others. Ultimately, I have developed the heart and soul of a doctor.

Our Assessment: This candidate used the statement to explain her greatest weakness, which is her introverted nature. By addressing it cleverly in the opening paragraph, and by describing her deliberate efforts to overcome her shyness by extending herself to other people, the candidate revealed a level of insight that few of her peers possessed. As an added bonus, two of her recommendation letters praised this metamorphosis, which confirmed her fit for a medical career.

Passion for Research

As a child, I was fascinated by the physical mechanisms that controlled our household appliances. In my free time, I perused a book entitled *How Things Run*, which explained the inner workings of radios, televisions, and computers. Afterwards, I applied my newfound knowledge by breaking apart the majority of my toys and re-assembling them. By the time I was a teenager, no appliance or device was too complex for me to understand.

At the same time, I was also intrigued by the subtle nuances of human behavior, which motivates the things that we say and do. As I walked through the hallways in high school, I pondered the many differences among my eclectic group of friends. Why did we enjoy certain subjects, but loathe others? Why did we each have a different sense of humor? And how would we make the thousands of decisions, both large and small, that would determine our life paths? These curiosities, combined with my ongoing love of mechanisms, fueled my passion for classes such as biology and psychology, which explained the physical and emotional aspects of life. They also made me more accepting of individual quirks and differences, which are an essential part of human diversity.

In college, I noticed that few people shared my dual passion for the physical and social sciences. Further, I recognized that these differences ultimately guided our choice of major and career. Most science enthusiasts gravitated to opportunities in physics and engineering, which made excellent use of their quantitative skills; likewise, the students in my psychology classes pursued options in social work and mental health counseling, which allowed them to connect with people. Unfortunately, for me, something seemed "missing" from both of these trajectories. The more I learned about science and human behavior, the more committed I became to *both* disciplines.

I finally realized that my dual passions were an excellent match for a medical career. To gain a realistic perspective of the profession, I took challenging science classes, worked countless hours as a volunteer, and completed a clinical research project at Cornell Medical Center. My honors thesis, which developed an implantable insulin pump for toddlers with diabetes, received the Chancellor's Medal for the Sciences in 2011. By working independently on this device, I gained practical experience planning and performing experiments, collecting results, and conducting literature searches in a dynamic new area. My results have been submitted for publication in the *Journal of Pediatric Medicine* and were recently presented as a poster abstract at a global medical conference. Additionally, I am currently preparing a US Patent application for the pump, with the help of the university attorney.

By working closely with doctors, nurses, psychologists, and researchers on my project, I enjoyed a level of personal and intellectual rigor that was not available in the classroom or laboratory. I also gained profound insight into how our bodies "work" and the complex factors that influence the disease process. After working extensively in a clinical environment, I realized that I love the diversity and challenges that the medical profession will provide.

To fulfill my role as a clinician, I am also completing a second degree in Communications, which will enhance my ability to interact with my future patients and colleagues. Although the challenges of completing a dual degree are immense, I have not allowed them to hinder my participation in activities that have helped me to mature as a person. Volunteering at a children's hospital has taught me important lessons about working with people, while playing chess has taught me the value of perseverance, dedication, and self-discipline. By exploring the non-academic parts of my personality, I have become a more compassionate person with a vibrant interest in the world around me. Eventually, this balance should also make me a more confident and responsive physician.

As a result of my experiences in the classroom, laboratory and hospital, I will bring enormous insight and passion to my studies in medical school. I will also bring my heartfelt commitment to this rigorous profession, which will enable me to use my scientific, interpersonal, and communication skills to help patients get well. On a daily basis, I can continue my lifelong quest to discover "how we work" in a way that benefits society. For me, there is no other choice than medicine.

Our Assessment: This candidate is a self-professed "science nut" who has published several papers and given numerous presentations at medical conferences. In this statement, he highlights the breadth of his interests, which have led him to a career in clinical medicine (rather than basic research). His lighthearted tone, particularly in the introductory paragraphs, allowed him to sell his strengths without sounding heavy-handed.

Candidate with Research Experience (PhD/MD)

While developing a vaccine for the human papillomavirus, which has recently been linked to cervical cancer, Dr. Janine Walker described medicine as "the final frontier," because insightful discoveries in basic research often lead to extraordinary innovations in health care. I have opted to pursue an MD/PhD program because I want to be part of this intriguing profession that allows such rigorous yet practical scientific exploration.

To learn about the clinical side of medicine, I volunteered at the St. Joseph's Hospital in Framingham throughout my four years of high school. While escorting patients from one test to another, I discovered the therapeutic effects of an encouraging smile and a friendly conversation. From observing patients with simple correctable problems, such as a broken arm, to those with chronic problems, such as diabetes, I gained an understanding of a physician's daily challenges. Each patient presented a unique array of symptoms that required specialized attention, including complex emotional needs. Amazingly, through their warmth and reassurance, the compassionate physicians at the hospital transformed their patients' fears into strength and hope.

In my freshman year of college, I explored my passion for biology by joining the genetics laboratory of Dr. Wayne Nelson. After learning about the biology of XXX, I decided to map its mechanism. With financial support from the John F. Kennedy Scholar Program, I cloned XXX-like elements that may cause the chromosomal rearrangements associated with age-dependent micro-nuclear degradation. The multitude of puzzles that I encountered in the laboratory challenged my creativity and fostered intellectual development that I could not achieve in a classroom. Additionally, by critically analyzing experimental obstacles, I gained invaluable problem solving skills. In my senior year, I will further investigate this intriguing model as part of my honors thesis.

This summer, I completed an internship that enhanced my understanding of the relationship between basic research and medicine. By working with Dr. Jill Bennett at the Beth Israel Cancer Center, I discovered the excitement that surrounds the emerging science and technology that will lead to future innovations in medicine. A long-term goal of Dr. Bennett's laboratory is to develop retroviral-mediated gene therapy for patients with chronic hemolytic anemia due to a severe deficiency of iron. I tested the efficiency of replication-defective retroviral vectors that are capable of transferring human gene to cells in vitro. By doing so, I hope to identify the specific mutation that causes inherited diseases such as cystic fibrosis and adenosine deaminase deficiency, which are currently incurable. Ideally, after I complete the MD/PhD program, I will be involved in both the primary care of these patients and the investigative research that leads to more effective therapies.

To me, medicine is not only the "final frontier," but the world's most vibrant and rewarding profession. At this point in history, our knowledge about the molecular aspects of medicine is growing each day. Through basic and clinical research, I hope to enhance our understanding of disease and provide the tools we will need to improve the lives of humans across the globe in a socially responsible manner.

<u>Our Assessment</u>: This candidate, who had a wealth of research experience, kept her statement clean and focused. By highlighting her passion for research and her clinical experience, she revealed the many skills that she will bring to the PhD/MD program.

Candidate for a Combination MD / PhD

I am interested in pursuing a combined MD/Ph.D. program because it is the best possible preparation for a career as a researcher in human genetics. While the Ph.D. program will help me to develop strong research skills, the MD program will provide me with knowledge of medicine from a "human" perspective that will allow me to conduct research of high social value. With a dual undergraduate degree in physics and psychology, I am confident that my academic background and research experience have adequately prepared me to complete such a demanding course of study.

During my sophomore year, I participated in the Science and Engineering Research Semester program at Argonne National Laboratory, which was sponsored by the Department of Energy. Thankfully, the dynamic environment at Argonne encouraged non-stop brainstorming and reflection. My work there, which involved data entry and analysis for cold fusion experiments, increased my familiarity with computer graphics and enhanced my understanding of nuclear fusion. Furthermore, it exposed me to the systematic problem-solving approach used by research physicists in attacking a problem. Although I was excited by the prospect of a career in scientific research, I was disenchanted with the possible social and military applications of my work.

I confirmed my distaste for weapons research the following fall, when I received a fellowship from Loyola's Family Foundation to devise and implement an after-school literacy program for elementary school children. The convivial nature of this job was the perfect complement to my experience at Argonne. Although I missed the intense academic environment at the research center, my fulfillment from working with the children reinforced my desire for socially meaningful work. At the suggestion of Mrs. Diane Carter, my supervisor at Loyola, I began to volunteer one day per week at Loyola Memorial Hospital. The therapeutic nature of helping patients opened my eyes to the world of possibilities for me in clinical medicine.

During the summer of 2007, I participated in the Undergraduate Research Program at the United States

Interdisciplinary Laboratory (USIL), which was sponsored by the National Science Foundation. I worked in the lab of Dr. Thomas Tyler, a computational biologist, and returned to his lab as a permanent employee after graduation. My objective at USIL is to determine the role of a specific seven-amino acid signal with an interesting pattern of distribution, including a tumor suppressor. My work involves writing and using computer programs for sequence analysis, reading technical papers, and conferring with other scientists at the lab. In addition, this experience has advanced my undergraduate computational training and expanded my knowledge of molecular and cell biology and genetics.

Working at USIL has been rewarding for a number of reasons. First, I enjoy the academic nature of the research and the intellectual atmosphere at the lab, particularly the social and medical implications of studying signal transduction in the cell. This project has also advanced my computational training and expanded my knowledge of molecular and cell biology and genetics. Finally, I have been fortunate to attend many meetings, lectures and conferences with my colleagues, including the 50th anniversary of Watson and Crick's discovery of the double helix structure of DNA. Participating in that celebration was a privilege that strongly reinforced my desire to pursue a career in a research environment.

Each of these experiences has helped me to determine what is important to me in choosing a career. I am particularly interested in the field of human genetics, and feel that combined MD/Ph.D. training will best prepare me to conduct competitive research with socially meaningful applications.

Our Assessment: Although heavy on technical details, this essay clearly summarizes the candidate's experiences and goals, which have inspired his application to a PhD/MD program. His recommendation letter from his supervisor confirmed his superior performance as a researcher, which made him an excellent fit for the program he chose.

Candidate with a PhD in Medical Research

As a child in India, my most vivid memory was visiting a village clinic that my father had helped to build. The sad faces of the sick children, whose diseases had no cure, haunted me for a long time. As the director of the clinic explained the concept of "medical research" to my father, I knew, inexplicably, that this intriguing field would be my professional calling. Indeed, for the past 10 years, I have devoted my life to medical research.

As an undergraduate student at the University of Bangalore, I originally thought that I would become a doctor. Frustrated by the focus on rote memorization, I shifted my focus to medical research, which allowed me to think independently while designing and conducting my own experiments. After completing my Master's degree in Immunology at the Indian Institute of Technology, I accepted a position as a researcher at the Stanford University Cancer Institute. In 2003, I was also appointed to a junior faculty position as an Instructor in Medicine at Stanford Medical School.

For the past twelve years, my research has focused in the field of transplantation immunology, including four years in the development of cancer vaccines and tumor immunology. As an investigator in our translational research program, I monitor the immune responses in patients with breast, renal, ovarian, melanoma and multiple myeloma who have been injected with individually-designed cancer vaccines in Phase I and Phase II clinical trials. I also investigate new strategies to enhance the potency of the cancer vaccines that could lead to the induction of more potent anti-tumor immune responses.

As a clinically oriented research program, we train medical students, residents, hematology/oncology fellows and attending oncology physicians in basic cancer research. Without a doubt, my greatest satisfaction has been teaching and mentoring these MDs, including visiting clinical fellows from Europe, Africa and the Far East. While supervising a group of undergraduate students, I was mesmerized by their passion for medicine. Their insightful questions and enthusiasm reawakened an aspect of my own professional dreams that had remained dormant for many years.

As one of the few non-physicians in our group, I have wrestled with the unsettling possibility that my lack of knowledge of clinical medicine diminishes my ability to teach and mentor. Unlike my trainees, who are medical students, residents, fellows and physicians, I do not interact with the patients in our clinical trials. As time has progressed, I have yearned to understand the emotional aspects of disease, which affect the body's ability to heal. With a medical degree, I would bring an added dimension to my research and would be a better mentor, teacher and supervisor to the next generation of clinical scientists. Furthermore, by adding a clinical qualification to my resume, I will be able to treat patients in a non-laboratory setting, which offers the potential for significant personal and professional rewards.

Ironically, most of the MDs that I mentor feel that they are deficient in the scientific aspect of our work, which is my area of expertise. They are always surprised to learn that I feel similarly handicapped because I am not clinically qualified. Although I have mastered many aspects of research, I have realized that I cannot thrive without the personal and professional fulfillment that a medical education will provide. After careful introspection, I have decided to address this handicap in a somewhat unorthodox manner; at age 33, I am heeding my childhood calling to become a physician.

As a seasoned researcher, I view my clinical training not as a detour from my path, but as a credential that will expand and complement my existing skills. I will bring several strengths to medical school, including my multicultural, educational and research experiences in India and Pakistan, along with my decade of scientific training and teaching experiences at Stanford. In my postdoctoral career, I have taught and mentored some of the most talented medical students and trainee physicians in the nation. Inspired by their example, I have realized that my maturity and insight will enhance what I bring to medicine, rather than detract from it. With the unqualified support of my family and peers, I am embarking on this journey with the same commitment and enthusiasm that have fueled my past endeavors. Nearly 20 years after visiting the village clinic in India, I am finally honoring my call to medicine.

Our Assessment: This candidate, who held a PhD in medical sciences, was a prolific researcher with nearly a decade of experience at a top medical school. In this statement, she explains her desire to augment her credentials with an MD. The statement was well received.

Chapter 4: Inspired by a Unique Life Experience

In their statements, many candidates discuss a unique or defining experience that helped to clarify their values. Ironically, the experience does not necessarily have to be a positive one; many times, we learn the greatest life lessons from the challenges and obstacles we face. A common sense caveat, however: if you choose to discuss a difficult experience, be sure to explain how you have learned and grown from it as a person. Your goal is not to elicit sympathy, but to position yourself as a survivor who has much to offer the medical school that accepts you.

Here are several successful answers to this question from candidates who were admitted to medical school. By design, we have grouped the statements in the following sub-categories:

Inspired by an Illness or Traumatic Experience
Inspired by Religion
From a Family of Physicians
Inspired by Immigration & Travel

To protect the privacy of the writer, the names of all people, classes, schools, places, teams, activities, and companies have been changed.

Inspired by an Illness or Traumatic Experience

There's always a long line of people waiting on the corner of Fifth Street and Washington Boulevard in downtown Boston. Although they look like tourists, they are actually donors who provide the "gift of life" to the District 32 Blood Bank. I have volunteered there since I was 18 years old, when a violent car accident changed my life. Unfortunately, while driving home from school, the bang that I heard wasn't just in my mind, but the sound of a motorcycle hitting my car at 35 mph. Its driver, a kid named Wyatt, was thrown onto a lawn more than 25 feet away. He was badly injured, but was fortunately wearing a helmet. I waited with him until the ambulance came, which was the longest 23 minutes of my life.

Thankfully, my injuries were minor because my car absorbed the bulk of the impact. But Wyatt was another story. His legs and arms were scraped beyond belief; he also had a terrible gash on his right leg that was bleeding profusely. Although Wyatt's injuries were not life-threatening, he needed multiple surgeries to stop his internal bleeding. The hospital faced an immediate dilemma because Wyatt's blood type, A positive, was in short supply. They were desperate for donors.

Although I wasn't a match, my father immediately stepped forward to donate, along with several hospital employees. Accidents like ours were a painful reminder of the urgent need for donors. Within an hour, two reporters from local news stations came to film a segment requesting blood donations. Although I declined to be interviewed about the accident, I was impressed by the hospital's quick call to action and the public's overwhelming response to help an injured boy.

The long-term effects of the accident were overwhelmingly positive. Wyatt recovered from his injuries, survived three months of rehabilitation, and gave up his motorcycle. He is currently in college in California, where he is studying to be a physical therapist. I began my volunteer work at the Blood Bank just six months after the accident and haven't missed a weekend shift in the past four years. I do every task that doesn't require a medical degree, including interviewing donors, taking medical histories, cataloging and transporting blood, and maintaining our computer records. I particularly enjoy interacting with the donors, who are kind and giving people who want to help their fellow humans. As a volunteer, I help our donors overcome their fears of needles, AIDS, passing out and developing anemia. I enjoy the role of teacher, which requires me to debunk rumors about donating blood and put people's minds at ease.

My rewarding experiences with the blood bank have inspired me to choose a career as a physician, which will allow me to make a lasting difference in my patients' lives. Talented young people like Wyatt are alive today because the dedicated doctors at Boston University Medical Center had the skills and technology to save him. Eventually, I hope to have the credentials I will need to make a similar contribution to society. At the very least, I can be a voice of hope and inspiration during life's most moments.

Our Assessment: This statement was effective because it explained the candidate's commitment to the Blood Bank, which sparked his decision to pursue a career in medicine. Combined with his recommendation letters, which documented his volunteer work, the candidate presented a highly impressive application.

Inspired by Mother's Illness

Three years ago, a malignant brain tumor destroyed my mother's pituitary gland. As recently as 1990, her cancer would have been a death sentence, but, thanks to the amazing breakthroughs in medical research, my mother is still here with us. Twice a day, she takes a genetically engineered growth hormone to replace the secretions that her body can no longer produce naturally. This miraculous technology has given back to her a portion of what she lost to the tumor.

One of the biggest innovations in medicine has been the use of bacteria to genetically engineer drugs such as insulin and growth hormone. For patients like my mother, they have literally made the difference between life and death. Current research suggests that growth hormone might also be an effective treatment for ailments as diverse as osteoporosis, severe burns and infertility. As a witness to its benefits, I am a staunch supporter of its research and development. Yet, to no one's surprise, there is a dark side to its availability and use.

Although many people could benefit from growth hormone, it can also be abused for athletic purposes. Football great Lyle Alzado appeared on national television to ask the public to refrain from misusing growth hormones, which he believed were responsible for his brain cancer. Before his death, he urged Congress to limit the availability of the drug to ensure that it does more good than harm. Mr. Alzado also asked the government to stop funding any type of related genetic research.

I respectfully disagree with his position. This research has allowed scientists to locate genes that are linked to diseases such as cystic fibrosis, sickle cell anemia and Huntington's disease. Eventually, this knowledge could yield better treatments or even a cure for these disorders. I cannot imagine anyone finding fault with important discoveries that can potentially save lives; to me, their benefits to society far outweigh the potential for abuse.

Throughout the 20th century, nearly every aspect of modern medicine has reaped the rewards of technological advancements, which are growing at an exponential rate. Every door we open leads to more doors, which may contain secrets as well as revelations. Granted, with every gain comes the possibility of abuse, but this does not justify ending an entire research program. The majority of the population can only imagine the excitement of opening one of these docrs for the first time. They know in their hearts that it could be *their* loved one who benefits from the resulting technology. In my mind, the answer is not stopping this research – or closing these doors, but properly regulating it to ensure its optimal implementation. The potential benefits to people like my mother are too significant to dismiss.

Throughout this journey, I learned more about the disease process, the promise of new technologies, and my own desire to play a role in their development, testing, and use. Fortunately, my family's battle had a happy ending; my mother went into remission and my darkest fears did not materialize. Nevertheless, her strength and courage remain a constant source of inspiration to me. By watching my mother cheat death and retain her faith in God, I have come to share her confidence that we will greet the future with a shared sense of hope and optimism. My fondest wish is that other families enjoy the amazing breakthroughs that God has provided for us. With the work of dedicated researchers – and progressive and compassionate laws regarding experimental drug protocols, they can.

Our Assessment: This statement eloquently and persuasively presents the candidate's position on the off-label use of growth hormones, which saved her mother's life. It also revealed her motivation to enroll in medical school and conduct groundbreaking research in this area.

Inspired by Brother's Illness

In difficult times, I am reminded of Friedrich Nietzsche's quotation, "What does not destroy me, makes me stronger." Ironically, when my family moved from Pakistan to the United States in 1999, I did not realize the many challenges I was about to face. On the surface, we were a typical immigrant family that was adjusting to life in a new culture. Blessed with good jobs and a solid marriage, my parents were determined to provide my brother and me with a promising future. Sadly, their love and support were no match for the insidious problem that invaded our home: my older brother's battle with schizophrenia, which began when he was 17 years old.

In hindsight, my brother's illness was not just a family crisis, but a turning point in my childhood. At age 13, when other girls were obsessed with clothes and boys, I was overwhelmed by the many problems that accompanied my brother's diagnosis. In addition to his illness, he also abused illegal drugs, which made his behavior more dangerous and erratic. My brother's problems soon became the sole focus of our family's energy, as my parents invested all of their resources to help him get well. Unfortunately, their efforts became increasingly futile. As my brother continued to refuse treatment, my father became severely depressed and was forced to file for bankruptcy. My mother became a workaholic, which left little time and energy for my needs. On an emotional level, I felt like I was completely alone.

Yet, as Nietzsche predicted, I ultimately became stronger and more focused by surviving this trauma. At a young age, I understood that bad choices could have devastating implications. In our family, my brother's decisions to consume illegal drugs and to refuse psychiatric treatment forced me to assume an adult role in our family far sooner than I was ready to do so. When I was 15, I accompanied my mother to bail my brother out of jail. To our horror, he had been placed in an isolation cell because he had attempted suicide the previous night. Amazingly, I somehow managed to survive a level of dysfunction that no child should be forced to endure.

As I matured, I became obsessed with the concept of personal responsibility. Although I loved my brother, the ramifications of his poor choices were a powerful incentive for me to make better decisions in my own life. With no external prodding, I became a willful young woman who was determined to achieve. Each time we moved, I adapted quickly to my new surroundings and excelled in the classroom. I fought hard to become responsible, respected and reliable. During times of crisis, I was the rational one who could solve problems and provide support for those who were paralyzed by grief and fear. Although I was just a teenager, I was already a survivor.

When I returned to Pakistan in 2005, I began to plan for the future. Despite my lack of funds, I completed my degree in psychology and accepted a position as a therapist in a home for troubled children. I was humbled to meet dozens of families that struggled with the same illness as my brother. By working closely with them, I discovered the importance of early diagnosis and treatment for disorders such as schizophrenia, which tend to emerge in the teenage years. I also discovered the effectiveness of several experimental drugs, which suppress the symptoms of the illness with minimal side effects. Had these medications been available when my brother was younger, he might have enjoyed a happier and more successful future.

After working in a clinical environment for the past three years, I have realized that I will never be fully satisfied in my career as a therapist. Instead, I want to become a physician who finds viable ways to treat and researches psychiatric illnesses that currently have no cure. By doing so, I can transform a negative experience into a positive one – and help other families avoid the trauma that mine has endured.

Sadly, for many survivors of mental illness, their only legacies are grief and shame. Fortunately, I have avoided such a dismal fate. By helping my parents weather an emotional storm, I developed the tools to tackle the inevitable challenges that life presents. I also developed a strong internal compass that guides all aspects of my personal and professional behavior. After coming so far, I am eager to embrace the challenges of medical school, where I will bring a vibrant perspective to discussions about mental illness. I will also bring the strength and tenacity of a survivor, who is determined to give back to society by becoming a physician of integrity and skill.

Our Assessment: This essay is risky because it reveals considerable information about the candidate's childhood, which was admittedly difficult. Nevertheless, by explaining how those experiences made her a stronger and more effective person, the author turned the essay into a masterful piece that showcases her personal strengths. Combined with her recommendation letters, which confirmed her effectiveness in stressful situations, the candidate's application was incredibly powerful.

Inspired by a Relative's Illness

My uncle, Adam Merolla, was my best friend in the world. For the first ten years of my life, we took a brisk walk to the park every afternoon, all bundled up in our down coats and thick woolen gloves. Along the way, I shared my dreams for the future, while Uncle Adam told me stories from his past. Finally, when we reached the park, he pushed me so high on the swings that I thought I might actually fly. Hours later, as we wandered back home, my Aunt Ginny sat at the kitchen table with two cups of cocoa for us. It is a simple memory, and all I have left of my Uncle Adam.

When I was in the seventh grade, my uncle was diagnosed with colon cancer. After his surgery, my mother received a call from his doctor with the worst news of my life. Although the surgeon had removed the tumor from my uncle's colon, the cancer was not treatable because it had metastasized to his liver. At most, the doctor believed that he would be with us for another six months.

In that brief moment, my entire world fell apart. I couldn't begin to absorb the devastating implications of my uncle's diagnosis. Ironically, I remembered all of the times that I had told him that I wanted to become a doctor. Suddenly, my goal had a powerful new meaning. I finally understood the feelings that accompanied popular cliches such as "life is short" and "time is fleeting." In an instant, my previous worries about my upcoming biology test and my first school dance seemed immature and trivial. My beloved uncle, who loved me without reservation, had cancer. How could I possibly live without him?

In hindsight, my uncle's diagnosis confirmed my calling to medicine and provided my first experience as a caregiver. Although my family could not cure his disease, we were determined to cherish whatever time we had left with him. Immediately after his surgery, Uncle Adam came to live with us, with the assistance of a hospice nurse. Suddenly, our roles were reversed, and I was determined to provide my uncle with the same level of care that he had always given me. On his good days, I played by his bedside and entertained him with stories about school. We caught every Red Sox game on television, in order to indulge my uncle's loyalty to the team. By making him laugh, I eased his suffering and helped him forget about the pain. Most importantly, throughout his last months, my uncle always knew he was loved.

Amazingly, despite his dire prognosis, my uncle retained his kindness and optimism until his last breath. His ability to display such fortitude solidified my desire to become a doctor; it also set a wonderful example for me to emulate. Since my uncle's death, I have channeled all of my energy into preparing for medical school, completing my Chemistry degree at Brown University and volunteering in the oncology ward at Rhode Island Hospital. Throughout my experiences, I try to provide all of my patients with the same level of compassionate care that I gave Uncle Adam.

Sadly, my uncle's death also taught me the hardest lesson of all; I cannot save everyone. As a doctor, I will eventually face the same challenge as the surgeon who delivered the terrible news about my uncle's prognosis. Undoubtedly, my heart will break for every patient I lose, who was someone's beloved parent, child and friend. Yet, being a physician will not make me God or even Superman, just a human who is determined to use my skills to comfort the sick and ease their suffering. I cannot imagine a more fulfilling use of my talents and skills.

People of faith believe that they are never alone, because God carries them through the roughest parts of their journey. After watching my uncle die in the loving serenity of our home, I concluded that no one should ever feel alone during life's hardest times. As an oncologist, I will help to carry those who are suffering through the worst parts of their journey. I am certain, on every level of my being, that this is the destiny that God has selected for me. Of all the dreams that I shared with Uncle Adam, I hold this one dearest to my heart.

Our Assessment: Many candidates write about death and illness in their families, but few of them do it as successfully as this applicant. By focusing exclusively on his relationship with his uncle, he showed the committee that he understood the personal aspects of illness from the patient's perspective. The statement perfectly complemented the rest of his application, which highlighted his academic and research accomplishments. Rather than repeat that material in the essay, the candidate revealed a part of his soul.

Inspired by Grandparent's Illness

I will never forget the look on my sister's face; her mouth dropped, her skin turned white and she clasped her hands in horror. At age 10, I was a six years older than Shannon – and comfortable with the bizarre site of Grandpa Joe's false teeth. Yet he always made a dramatic display of removing them in front of his grandchildren for the first time. Shannon, of course, gave him reaction he expected, which Grandpa still talks about with glee. To this day, I don't think that Shannon has ever forgiven him for frightening her that way.

Ironically, that event with Grandpa Joe forced me to view the situation more maturely. For the first time, I wondered why and when he had lost his natural teeth. Sadly, I also wondered if it would happen to me. Would I someday wake up with a bunch of teeth on my pillow? If so, would there be any sort of warning? I asked Grandpa Joe several questions that night, to try to understand why he had lost crucial parts of his body. Since then, Grandpa Joe has consistently expressed the same sentiments: "You don't keep your teeth forever. At some point, they die and you get false ones."

Although I believed him, I never liked his pat explanation – or his sad resignation to ill health. I decided to explore the story more thoroughly and discover exactly why teeth got sick and died. In hindsight, it was my first serious interest in medicine. More than fifteen years later, I am still seeking answers to comparable medical questions.

Through my anatomy classes, I discovered that the answer is preventive health, for both teeth and the rest of our bodies. My grandfather's generation didn't have the necessary information to care for their teeth and gums. If they had, fewer would have lost their natural dentition. Since then, I have discovered that the same premise applies to many other areas of medicine; the more information people have, the better health decisions they make. With that in mind, I am committed to a career as a public health physician, to disseminate quality information to the people who need it the most.

My undergraduate degree in nutrition has provided a wonderful background in both the hard and soft sciences; it has also given me valuable experience as a teacher and peer counselor at the college health center. For my internship, I worked with a group of 20 young women who had had successfully completed a 30-day inpatient program for eating disorders at the University of Kansas Medical Center. Upon their return to the university, they participated in an interdepartmental support program to develop and maintain a nutritious diet plan. As a teacher and counselor, I coordinated weekly group meetings at which the girls discussed their challenges in sticking with the plan and avoiding their temptations to starve, binge or purge.

This program was an epiphany for me. I discovered that eating disorders are insidious and never truly "cured." During our group therapy sessions, we worked diligently to identify the stressors and establish a support system for each girl. Although they know that this battle will literally last a lifetime – and offers no guarantees, they have all expressed considerable gratitude for the support we have provided them. I am honored to be part of it.

I have chosen XXX Medical School because of your exceptional reputation in public health administration and education. As part of my medical school experience, I want to obtain comprehensive training in disease prevention and treatment; ideally, I also want to become a skilled communicator who can disseminate health information to patients in an effective manner. According to current studies, most common diseases are easier to treat if they are diagnosed early, while others can be prevented if the appropriate risk factors are known and publicized. I can't turn back the clock and give my grandfather's generation their natural teeth back, but I will devote my career to educating the public about other serious diseases, such as AIDS, cancer, stroke, and hepatitis, which can be prevented with effective education programs. Although I cannot change the world, I am committed to saving one patient at a time, every day of my life.

Our Assessment: Initially, this candidate struggled to create a first draft that conveyed her early interest in medicine. Her introductory story about her grandfather's teeth was sweet and memorable; it also served as a natural springboard to her subsequent discussion about her education and volunteer work.

Motivated by Brother's Illness (PhD/MD Candidate)

Before I learned that my older brother was HIV-positive, I thought that AIDS was only a threat to people who were homosexuals or intravenous drug users. The virus, and the people who were afflicted with it, seemed as distant as the continent where the disease had originated. Brian's diagnosis forced me to open my mind to a risk that had previously seemed infinitesimal. Eventually, my obsession to learn more about HIV fueled my desire to become a physician.

A year after Brian returned to our family home, I enrolled at Temple University as a Biology major. I was desperate to learn how and why his body's processes had gone awry. Through a series of challenging honors courses, I learned that the human body is exquisitely complex, but controlled by an underlying theme of systems. That was reassuring to me. Even if I didn't know all of the molecules and connections, I couldn't deny that a fundamental order existed.

From physiology to cell biology to molecular genetics, my classes presented smaller and smaller systems to explain the origins of disease. Finally, when I studied the innocuous four letter alphabet of genes, I understood the foundation of human life. My two summers at Argonne National Lab gave me the opportunity to identify the gene that caused X-linked severe combined immunodeficiency (SCID). Although AIDS and SCID are different diseases (SCID is exclusively hereditary), they both compromise the body's defense mechanisms against foreign pathogens. Since SCID was a distant cousin of AIDS, I felt this was a significant connection. Learning about the common themes among immunodeficiency disorders, such as the perils of opportunistic infections, helped me to begin to understand what had happened to Brian. In the SCID laboratory, and in classroom seminars on infectious diseases, science helped me to demystify the disease.

Brian, of course, gave the virus a human face that I simply could not ignore. On school vacations, I accompanied him to a support group for AIDS patients and their families. Within a short period of time, I began to volunteer at the center and moderate various discussion groups. During the school year at Temple, I also work as a volunteer counselor at an off-campus HIV clinic, where discussing the virus is a great way for visitors to release anxiety. It also greatly enhances the educational process, which is essential to stop the spread of the disease. As an HIV counselor at an anonymous clinic, I feel both the potential and limits of my role. Obviously, I can't monitor my clients' behavior, nor can I judge them when they make decisions that place them in obvious risk. Instead, I share the best information I have and hope that they use it accordingly.

Thanks to advancement in drug therapies such as AZT, Brian's condition has stabilized in the last few months and he has recently returned to college. Like me, he is passionate about helping people with the disease, although his focus in psychological, rather than medical. Brian's positive response to his medication has boosted my excitement about pursuing a medical degree. As the relative of an HIV patient, I am invigorated by each new development that brings hope to patients' lives. I cannot imagine a more fulfilling career than investigating new treatments for immunodeficiency disorders, such as AIDS and SCID.

Our Assessment: This candidate struggled to write this essay, due to its personal nature. In the end, he simply spoke from the heart. By becoming a doctor, he hopes to cure the disease that threatens his brother's life. His strong academic background, volunteer experiences, and success as a researcher made him a perfect fit for the medical school that admitted him.

Motivated by a Traumatic Life Experience

Twelve years later, I can still hear the deafening sounds in my ears. As government planes bombed a nearby village, two freedom fighters brought a wounded child to the field hospital where I volunteered. The smell of blood, smoke, and gunpowder filled the air and added to the oppressive humidity. Unfortunately, after a lifetime of violence along the border between Iran and Iraq, I was all too familiar with the consequences of this random carnage.

Throughout my childhood, I witnessed these horrific scenes on a daily basis, as the Iraqi army raided our community. At an age when other children were learning the alphabet, I had already acquired an extensive knowledge of weapons and military terminology. Many days, to avoid places that were targeted by snipers, we took several hours to get to our school. For those who did not live in the midst of random violence, our warped sense of "normalcy" was unfathomable.

Throughout the turmoil, my father was determined to make a better life for our family. In 2001, we abandoned our few possessions and fled to Saudi Arabia. Although we found physical safety there, we faced formidable struggles to find jobs, enroll in school and simply survive. When my father passed away in 2005, I came to San Diego with a one-way plane ticket and $200 in cash. By working several odd jobs, I was able to help my family in Iran and save money for an eventual visit. In America, I finally saw the possibility for a better life.

During a short visit to Iran in 2007, I was detained by the border guards, who were not inclined to let me return to the United States. Fortunately, with the help of a friend, I made a dramatic escape and was granted political asylum in the US. For the past five years, I have devoted my life to supporting my family and to pursuing my dream of becoming a doctor. With the competing demands of work and family, the road has not been easy. After completing my associate's degree at the Community College of San Diego, I dropped out of school several times before I completed my BA at the University of California-Los Angeles. Despite many challenges and setbacks, I have remained focused on my long-term goal.

Like many aspiring physicians, I always knew that medicine was my calling. Unlike many of my peers, however, my commitment to ease the suffering of others was inspired by my early exposure to violence. As a powerless child, my only sanity was my dream of somehow making a better life. My heroes during these years were the brave physicians in the field hospital who risked their own lives to save the injured. As a volunteer, I yearned to make a similar contribution.

Needless to say, I am not your typical medical school applicant. My most compelling credentials are not my GPA and MCAT scores, which suffered from my need to work while I completed school. Due to timing constraints, I actually took the MCAT before I had the chance to complete the requisite classes in Physics and Organic Chemistry. (My subsequent performance in these classes demonstrates my mastery of these subjects.) Despite my erratic academic history, I am justifiably proud of my achievements, which are tangible proof of my ability to perform under pressure. This trait has helped me to overcome seemingly insurmountable obstacles and will serve me well in medical school.

In addition to my work at the hospital in Iran, I have also volunteered for the American Red Cross and have tutored underprivileged children in California. Throughout these experiences, I have noted the chronic need for compassionate physicians to work in poor, underserved areas. Despite the affluence in the US, many inner city residents lack access to affordable health care. The prohibitive cost of basic screening tests for heart disease and cancer has increased the number of preventable deaths; the absence of pre-natal and well-baby care, including routine immunizations, is also troubling.

Following medical school, I plan to work as a general practitioner in an inner city setting, where I will provide compassionate care to a population whose needs are not being served. By implementing a comprehensive program in preventive medicine, I will help my patients live healthier lives. I also hope to volunteer with an organization such as Physicians Without Borders, which serves people in developing countries. After surviving my own tenuous childhood along the Iran/Iraq border, I am compelled to help those who cannot help themselves. In many ways, my tenacity is a positive legacy of the ongoing violence I observed. Regardless of the obstacles I face, I simply refuse to give up.

Our Assessment: This candidate's observations about his childhood in Iran were chilling. However, the committee was equally impressed by his tenacity in completing his education under difficult circumstances. Admittedly, the applicant's GPA and MCAT scores were disappointing; however, he submitted extraordinary recommendation letters from those who had supervised his work in a clinical setting – and confirmed his superior personal qualities. His overall application was very strong.

Inspired by an International Event

As the 12th grade biology class gathered around the demonstration table, the students giggled with excitement. After learning about the organ systems of the body, they were finally going to witness the dissection of a rabbit. Their youthful teacher, dressed in a white lab coat, briefly explained what he was about to do. After lifting the abdominal skin with a pair of forceps, he made a long vertical incision. Pulling back the ribcage, he exposed the animal's heart and lungs, taking care not to puncture any major blood vessels. The sight of the throbbing heart amazed the impressionable students, who tried to feel their own hearts beating. After pointing out various organ systems, the teacher closed the abdomen and ribcage with suture clips. Two girls congratulated him, saying "Sir, you should have been a doctor!"

I was that enthusiastic teacher, who had long harbored the dream of becoming a physician. My interest in medicine began in my bachelor's degree program at the University of Bangalore, where I conducted research under Dr. Pradip Patel on the parasitemia and immunological responses to *Trypanosoma* infections that cause the African sleeping sickness. During our week-long trip to the Kenyan coast, I watched the doctors at the International Children's Hospital use their skills to diagnose and treat diseases. I yearned to have their education and skills. Years later, as my biology students streamed out of the lab, I still hoped to bring my dream to fruition.

In hindsight, growing up in an underprivileged Indian community was a mixed blessing. Although my financial hardships hindered my ability to pay for school, they bolstered my determination to succeed. In our small village, where nearly everyone lacked proper health care, I became sensitive to the needs of the poor and vulnerable. I also developed a passion for biology, which explained not only the origin of illness, but how tadpoles turned into frogs. By becoming a teacher, I found a creative way to combine my love of science with my desire to help others. Throughout the years, as I taught biology at an international high school, I searched for a suitable opportunity to pursue a career in medicine.

While completing my master's degree in biology, the bombing of the American Embassy in New Delhi created an urgent need for medical personnel. I was frustrated by my inability to help my colleague, who lost his eye in the attack. To this day, I am humbled by my memories of the sick and needy victims, who begged for coins from total strangers. My motivation to become a physician was further strengthened during my stay in Africa, where I volunteered for an HIV/AIDS awareness campaign, alongside doctors and church leaders from the United States. As I lectured on the biology, clinical symptoms and statistics of HIV/AIDS, I learned about the educational opportunities in America. In addition to fueling my desire to become a doctor, the physicians I met at the conference encouraged me to come to the US.

Since 2006, I have worked on my doctorate in physiology at the University of Vermont, where I am also completing a concentration in public health. My most rewarding activity was volunteering at the University Hospital's ER, where I assisted the nurses and emergency technicians in their regular duties. Whenever possible, I worked directly with patients, who were delighted to learn that someone from across the globe was part of their medical team. My diverse clinical experiences, including exposure to pediatrics and orthopedic surgery, have given me a clear understanding of the challenges of the profession.

Throughout my life, I have overcome numerous obstacles to complete my PhD and embark on a career in medicine. By doing so, I have demonstrated the resilience required in such a demanding field. Additionally, my strong research background and my clear understanding of science will enhance my diagnostic skills. Eventually, I hope to use my talent for teaching to educate the public about the prevention and treatment of disease. By promoting the benefits of preventive medicine, I can make a positive difference in the world around me. I will also fulfill my personal destiny, which my biology students so graciously acknowledged; I will finally be a doctor.

Our Assessment: This candidate had a solid reputation as a teacher and researcher before he began his pursuit of a medical degree. In this statement, he offers a delightful introduction about his career as an educator, followed by a moving discussion of his volunteer endeavors in other nations. His application was well perceived.

From a Family of Physicians

With a gentle twist of his hand, my father removed the brittle bones in his patient's hip and replaced them with synthetic implants. From my seat in the observation room, I watched in awe as his surgical team closed the patient, leaving just a thin line of visible sutures. Until that moment, I didn't fully understand my father's passion for being a doctor. A few weeks later, when the 70-year-old patient walked without pain for the first time in years, I couldn't imagine doing anything else.

As part of a medical family, I was raised with a keen awareness of the challenges of delivering health care. Each summer, we visited my grandfather in Kenya, who was the only practitioner in his rural village. Ironically, as an orthopedic surgeon in North Dakota, my father faced similar problems as my grandfather in Kenya. Far too often, the poorest and sickest members of society do not have access to the technology that is needed to save them. This problem was a vibrant topic at our family dinner table, where my father often expressed his desire to champion a more equitable distribution of health care. In hindsight, my father gave me a fascinating perspective of the medical profession, but he never pressured me to join it. From his perspective, medicine was not a career choice, but a calling. Being a doctor was a lifelong commitment of his heart, mind and soul.

As an undergraduate student at Stanford University, I explored my early interest in sociology and the law by completing a liberal arts curriculum. Although I enjoyed my classes, my heart kept tugging me back to my childhood goal. During my junior year of college, I began to volunteer as an operating room liaison at Stanford Hospital, where I discovered that I enjoyed a clinical environment, including my work with patients. Over the Christmas holiday, I observed my father perform a hip replacement and a knee replacement, which solidified my decision to become a physician. Seeing my father's skill in the operating room, I was humbled to know that he was rebuilding his patients' bodies with his bare hands. Weeks later, he watched with pride as his patients took their first tentative steps back to health. Deep in my heart, I longed to pursue a career that would enable me to make a similar contribution to people's lives. I was finally ready to honor my call to medicine.

After graduating from Stanford, I decided to fulfill my medical school prerequisites as a post-baccalaureate student at the University of California at Davis. During this time, I also worked as a medical assistant at the ophthalmology practice of Dr. David Shaw, where I assisted with patient consultations and eye examinations. I am also researching and co-authoring an article with Dr. Shaw on a rare combination of eye conditions, which will be published in a medical journal. Yet my most satisfying experience was working as a health educator in Kenya, where I taught patients about HIV/AIDS awareness. As a volunteer for the Center for International AIDS Awareness (CIAA), I presented information in an imaginative way, using theatre and street plays to educate children and adults about this serious health matter. In such a high-risk region, health education was the only viable way to reduce the proliferation of this deadly virus.

Sadly, my motivation was temporarily shaken in 2009, after my father's unexpected death. Although my desire to become a doctor came from within, I was overwhelmed by the loss of such an inspirational parent and role model. Thankfully, as my grief subsided, I remembered my father's pride when I announced my decision to become a doctor. He would never want me to abandon my calling. Although my father will not be able to see the fulfillment of my goals, he provided a powerful example of compassion and integrity that will continue to guide my path.

Ten years from now, I hope to be a competent and caring physician who works in the public health care sector, providing quality care to patients who would not otherwise be served. I am particularly eager to continue my work in health education to prevent the spread of HIV/AIDS. Although I cannot save every patient, I am committed to using my skills as a clinician and researcher to help people live longer lives. By exploring different aspects of medicine, I have deepened my commitment to my goals and demonstrated my ability to handle diverse types of challenges. I am finally ready to fulfill my destiny, to become a physician of compassion and skill.

Our Assessment: This candidate came from a medical family, but he had never been pressured to join the profession. In this statement, he eloquently explains how he found his own path to a career in clinical medicine. Along the way, the candidate acquired impressive credentials that revealed his extraordinary preparation for the challenges ahead.

From a Medical Family

From the time I entered kindergarten, I already knew that I wanted to be a doctor. My father, who is a pediatrician, seemed astonished by my early fascination with the field. When I visited him at work, I was amazed by his ability to help his patients get well. My favorite picture of myself was taken at age 4, when I posed with an old stethoscope draped around my neck. Although my father encouraged me to pursue my own dreams, I couldn't imagine a more fulfilling career than medicine.

As I matured, I began to understand the profound obstacles that my father overcame to achieve his goals. When he was a child, my father's family moved from Rwanda to Egypt to escape the genocide. As an outsider in a foreign country, my father was not offered the same professional or educational opportunities that were available to native Egyptians. Rather than abandon his dream, he went to medical school in Saudi Arabia, where he studied by candlelight because the government turned off the electricity at 9 pm. Yet my father somehow found solace and friendship in this barren environment. Rather than return to Egypt after graduation, he remained in Saudi Arabia for several years to provide medical care at an understaffed clinic.

In 1991, my father returned to Rwanda to work as a general practitioner. Although he loved his patients, he feared for our family's future under the oppressive regime, which faced ongoing threats from warring tribes. In 1993, when I was just six years old, my entire family immigrated to the United States to pursue a better life. With just $150 in their pockets and three people to support, my parents faced formidable challenges, but they never regretted their decision. To them, the benefits of freedom were worth any personal or financial sacrifice they had to endure.

As a teenager, I watched with awe as my father re-built his career in middle age. Despite his obvious skills, my father was discouraged from obtaining a medical license in the US because he was "too old" and did not speak a word of English. Nevertheless, he refused to be deterred. While working nights as an orderly, my father mastered English and studied for his licensing exams at night. Afterwards, he endured many difficulties in his residency because people could not understand his thick accent, yet he still refused to give up. Whatever challenge my father faced, he came up with a plan to conquer it. Medicine was his calling, and he refused to abandon it.

Thanks to my family's sacrifices, my premedical studies have been significantly less stressful than my father's. As a high school student in San Diego, I joined the med-science program and took double periods of biology. I was immediately attracted to the challenges of a science curriculum, which required a healthy balance of analytical and logical thinking. Rather than simply answer our questions, my teacher encouraged us to think through the problem and find our own solution. Further, through my participation in the honors program, I learned how to conduct and document original research.

My most fulfilling activity was participating in the medical ethics group, which discussed controversial medical issues and the laws that govern them. We also debated past court cases and the decisions that affect how health care is administered. By participating in the group, I gained a new perspective of the challenges that physicians face to develop care plans for their patients. I also became sensitive to opposing viewpoints on controversial issues.

As a high school student, I began a rewarding series of jobs in the medical field. First, I worked in the office of an internist, where I did clerical work and took patient histories. As a college student, I watched the recovery process from start to finish when I worked with elderly stroke patients at a rehabilitation clinic. As I bathed them and changed their sheets, they shared their amazing stories of surviving the Great Depression and serving in the war. I treasured the bond that I formed with each patient, which was a tangible reminder of the role of compassion in medicine.

Despite the demands of my outside jobs, I graduated from the University of San Diego with a dual degree in biology and psychology in 2009. Since then, I have worked as a community liaison for the California State Assembly, where I help my clients obtain jobs, medical care, and affordable child care. Although I derive tremendous satisfaction from this work, I miss the joy of clinical medicine. When I consider the future, I am constantly reminded of the challenges that my father faced to make his dreams come true. Thanks to his positive example, I share not only his passion for medicine, but the willingness to do whatever is necessary to achieve my goals.

As I embark on my medical career, I am deeply appreciative of the opportunities I have enjoyed because I live in the United States. I am honored to give back to the community that has nurtured my hopes and dreams. As a physician, I will deliver compassionate care that treats the whole person, not just a symptom or disease. I will keep abreast of new developments to ensure that each patient enjoys the best possible chance for recovery. Thanks to my father's fine example, I possess the stamina to handle the rigors of such a rewarding and challenging career. Regardless of the obstacles I face, I will not abandon my goal.

Our Assessment: This statement, although long, tells the candidate's fascinating story as the child of a physician in a war-torn country, who had to re-build his practice from scratch in a new nation. The applicant's diverse experiences, combined with his keen motivation and insight, made him an excellent fit for several top programs.

From a Family of Physicians

On the evening of my high school graduation, my father invited me to join him on our back porch while he leisurely smoked a Brazilian cigar. The house was filled with family, friends and other well-wishers; consequently, I suspected that my father's invitation to leave the party was really an invitation for us to talk in private. I wasn't wrong. As he slowly inhaled the burning leaves of his cigar, my father reminisced about his college days at Princeton. He was delighted that I was enrolling at his alma mater and that I would be a fourth-generation Walker legacy. Dad proceeded to note that every generation of Walker men had chosen medicine as a career and had become a successful physician. He obviously expected me to do the same.

I didn't respond to my father's words that night. Instead, upon my arrival at Princeton, I quietly investigated alternative career possibilities. My freshman trip with the campus choir suggested that I had other talents that were worth nurturing. While traveling through Europe, I toured and performed at more than 30 historical cathedrals. During this two-month whirlwind, I constantly checked my language guide in order to converse with people in each new city. When I returned home, I had never felt as happy or energized; I began to think that a career in music, international relations, or languages might be in the cards.

When I returned to Princeton, I avoided science courses in favor of advanced offerings in music, literature and the classics. Although I enjoyed my classes, I missed the analytical challenges and mathematical rigor of biology and chemistry. Occasionally, I found myself reading my roommate's copy of *Lancet*, the British medical journal. During our late-night debates on stem cell research, I wondered if I would eventually be drawn back to the field that my ancestors so warmly embraced.

My two subsequent summers in a chemistry lab rekindled my love of the sciences. To challenge my skills, I accepted a position as a teaching assistant in biology at the University of Milan. What an exhilarating experience! I was delighted to have the chance to perfect my fluency in Italian in such a rewarding way.

While immersed in my new culture, I also volunteered in a local hospital, where I provided comfort measures to pediatric patients. I was gratified by the appreciation I received from both my patients and students. Slowly, over my delightful summer, I realized that medicine was my true calling, which would allow me to connect with people in a deep and special way. Many of my patients were within a few years of my age, yet they respected my knowledge and experience. They trusted me to help them, and I thrived in my role as caregiver, teacher and friend.

My subsequent years at Princeton were filled with typical pre-medical frenzy: anatomy labs, biochemistry quizzes and endless nights grading papers. I loved every second of the challenging curriculum. In stressful times, I considered the complex combination of skills that my father and grandfather use every day as physicians: their jobs require them to simultaneously be a helper, teacher, scientist and sleuth. Unlike other career choices, medicine will push all of my buttons by combining my love of people, science, research and teaching. I also acknowledge the irony of my decision. Without one push from my well-meaning dad, I concluded that medicine was "in the blood" of another generation of Walker men. The decision is completely mine, as it should be. Medicine will continually challenge me to help others remain healthy so they can pursue their own dreams. I can't imagine anything else I would rather do.

<u>Our Assessment</u>: Candidates from medical families face a unique dilemma in the admissions process. On one hand, the committee knows that they understand the commitment that is required to succeed in the profession because they have observed it in their own household. On the other hand, they may question whether or not the decision to become a doctor is truly the candidate's.

This statement, although casually written, conveyed the writer's determination to follow his own professional path. On a competitive basis, the committee respected his decision to follow his heart and explore alternative fields before he made this commitment. It removed any doubt about whether or not he was being pushed into this profession by his father.

From a Family of Physicians

William Hazlitt, the renowned English writer, once said, "Prosperity is a great teacher; adversity is a greater." Over the years, I have endured a number of obstacles that have tested my character and motivation. In the aftermath of September 11, I was the victim of a hate crime. Days later, I was diagnosed with celiac disease, which is a biological intolerance to gluten. At the time, I thought that my misfortunes were the toughest I would ever endure. Yet my first year of college brought an unbearable loss that continues to shape my life—the death of my beloved father.

When I completed my last final, I looked forward to relaxing with my family and friends. I did not know that my parents were keeping a devastating secret about my father's health. As soon as I arrived home, I learned that he had been hospitalized earlier that week. I cried helplessly when I entered my father's room; the vivacious man that I knew and loved had been replaced by a frail stranger who barely had the strength to speak. Desperate to help, I offered to donate half of my liver to him; as a surgeon, my father was intimately familiar with the transplant procedure. Sadly, time was not my friend. For several days, I could do nothing but sit loyally by his side.

Miraculously, by the end of the week, my father's situation began to show promise: he was the first patient on the liver transplant list; a helicopter was prepared to airlift him to another hospital; and most importantly, his lab results began to improve. Upon hearing the news, my entire family rejoiced. We even mused about the possibility of my father writing a book about his experience to inspire others. Looking back, we were blinded by a sense of hope, which was quickly snatched away. Without warning, my father's pulse dropped to zero; we watched in agony as his physicians tried to revive him. With the simple words, "I am sorry. He is gone," our lives were permanently changed.

Although I enjoy challenges, I was overwhelmed by the ones that accompanied my father's death. In accordance with Islamic culture, I was asked to assume his role and responsibilities in our family. Suddenly, I was no longer the youngest of three, who was living the carefree college life; my mother and siblings were depending on me for leadership and support. While the rest of my family mourned our loss, I suppressed my own emotions in a haze of activity. Within 24 hours, I arranged my father's funeral, organized our finances and spread the news to our friends and family members. In subsequent weeks, I assumed the responsibility for dozens of matters, both large and small, for which I had little knowledge or preparation. Despite my calm demeanor, the stress began to take its toll; I developed a persistent case of insomnia, which left me even more exhausted.

Looking back, the past three years have been a time of tremendous growth, both personally and academically. Although I have struggled at times to piece my life back together, I have refused to let my father's death derail my hopes and dreams. Instead, I have slowly come to terms with my intangible qualities, which will help me to achieve my goals. By assuming responsibility at a young age, I have learned to set priorities and balance my personal and academic endeavors. With my siblings scattered across the country and my mother's health slowly deteriorating, I have learned to cherish every moment with them as a true blessing. Most importantly, I have realized that whatever challenges the future may bring, I will face them with honor, strength and integrity. I will not fail.

When I look to the future, I am reminded of my father's unwavering faith in me; he always told me that I could do anything, if I simply worked hard enough. In the aftermath of his death, I have been buoyed by his sense of optimism. By surviving a trying time with grace and persistence, I have deepened my perspective of what I can I accomplish in life. Like my father, I am committed to helping sick people get well. My childhood dream of becoming a surgeon is an ambitious goal that will enable me to make a meaningful contribution to my colleagues, family and community. With the lessons I have learned in the past three years, I will embrace the challenges of medical school with focus and dedication; I will become the man my father always knew I could be.

Our Assessment: On a literary basis, this statement is lovely; it opens with a strong quote, followed by a memorable story about the candidate's loss of his father. However, this essay was also risky, because it did not discuss his credentials for medicine, which were quite impressive; he had a top GPA, significant research experience, and clinical experience at a hospital in Israel. Thankfully, the committee learned about those accomplishments from the candidate's recommendation letters and activity list, which discussed them in detail. In the end, his decision to write about a more personal topic paid off.

Inspired by Childhood Illness and International Relocation

As the child of an American soldier and a Vietnamese mother, I was raised by my maternal grandparents in the harsh conditions of post-war Vietnam. After the fall of Saigon, we struggled to adjust to life with a communist government and a new political party, which deprived us of food, water and medical care. Unfortunately, I suffered from rheumatic fever, which required a level of medical intervention that was unavailable in an undeveloped country like Vietnam. As my diseased heart grew progressively worse, it interfered with my ability to perform my normal daily activities.

Through the Amer-Asian Relief Program, I came to the United States as a refugee in 2001. After my arrival, a team of American doctors successfully replaced my mitral valve and restored my health. My exposure to American medicine opened my eyes to the wonders that a compassionate physician can achieve. Initially, I was overwhelmed by the hospital and the flurry of activity around me, yet the medical staff worked around the clock to keep me safe and comfortable. The residents, in particular, took extra time to listen to my needs and concerns. With their compassionate care, I recovered quickly and confidently. Inspired by their example, I decided to pursue a medical career, to provide exceptional service to patients in a respectful manner.

I have subsequently worked in a series of medical positions to gain different perspectives of the profession. As a technician in a research laboratory, I learned proper lab technique, organizational skills and how to prioritize projects. As a cardiology technician, I helped the doctors to perform treadmill tests on patients with acute heart disorders; I was honored to share my experiences as a cardiac patient with them. In my current position as an anesthesia technologist, I help to deliver anesthesia to patients before surgery. These positions have given me a unique opportunity to connect with people on an emotional level, which is the most powerful gift that a physician can offer.

On a practical basis, my clinical experiences have taught me how to deliver compassionate and culturally sensitive care that honors the needs of each individual patient. From working in different departments, I have also gained an appreciation for the team approach to medicine, in which every person must do his part to ensure a positive outcome. In difficult times, I often draw upon my emotional strengths as well as my clinical skills. From my childhood memories of hospitalization, I understand what patients feel and what they need. Even simple gestures, such as getting a tissue for their tears and carefully explaining a procedure, can greatly reduce their anxiety. Often, simply holding a patient's hand will help to alleviate his stress and make him feel better.

Recently, I expanded my skills by volunteering at a nursing home that serves a large Asian population, including a number of people from my native village in Vietnam. I obtain indescribable joy from working with them, refreshing my language skills, and exploring aspects of the Asian culture that would otherwise be lost. By sharing their experiences with me, my patients have opened my eyes to aspects of life, history, culture, and suffering that I could never have learned from my textbooks. Sadly, they have also exposed me to the reality of medicine, which cannot cure every patient.

Nevertheless, medicine challenges me on a personal and intellectual level; every patient is different, which presents unexpected challenges to the health care team. After medical school, I hope to complete a residency in cardiology and build a practice repairing heart defects such as the one that I was born with; I want to master the intricate surgical techniques that will allow me to repair and replace the human heart. Few other specialties require such a complex integration of scientific, clinical, surgical and interpersonal skills. I am eager to develop those skills to make the maximum contribution to medicine.

Ideally, I can also divide my time between the two countries that I am proud to call home – the United States and Vietnam. By building my practice in the US, I can stay abreast of the latest developments in the field, which utilize state-of-the-art surgical and pharmaceutical technologies. At the same time, I will support the work of humanitarian groups such as Doctors without Borders, which bring essential services to underserved communities. Without the compassionate assistance of the Amer-Asian Relief Program, I would not have survived my illness, moved to the United States, or met my father's family. I would be honored to use my skills to pay forward these blessings to other deserving patients.

Our Assessment: This essay, although long, tells the candidate's emotional story about surviving a life-threatening illness and joining his father's family in the United States. More importantly, he explains his commitment to cardiology, which will allow him to treat other patients with heart defects. After reviewing his academic and professional accomplishments, the committee knew that the candidate had the intelligence, drive, and character to transform his dreams into reality.

Chapter 5: Older & Non-Traditional Candidates

Although most medical school applicants are recent college graduates, some are significantly older than their peers, with advanced degrees and several years of work experience. For these candidates, the personal statement is a golden opportunity to update the committee on what they have accomplished since they graduated from college. Ideally, the statement should also explain the type and extent of your professional experiences and how they have influenced your goals.

Additionally, the committee will may wonder why you are seeking a medical degree after working for many years in another profession. If you can provide this insight in your personal statement, the admissions committee will be able to confirm your personal and professional fit for a medical career.

Here are several excellent personal statements from older and non-traditional candidates who gained admission to highly competitive medical schools. To protect the privacy of the candidate, the names of all people, classes, schools, places, teams, and companies have been changed.

Older Candidate – Experience in Social Services

As the dilapidated Jeep made its way along the dirt road, I finally caught a glimpse of the lush African landscape. Our destination was Jutta, a tiny village two hundred miles north of Zambia, where telephones, running water and electricity were completely unavailable. As a freshman at Duke University, I was part of a multinational team that was spending the summer in Africa on a medical development project. The trip to Jutta was my first jaunt outside the United States, much less to a third world area. For a brief second on that dirt road, I wondered if I had been kidding myself about my ability to make a difference in the world.

Fortunately, once we reached the makeshift clinic, we managed to establish a moderate degree of normalcy. From eight o'clock each morning until six o'clock in the evening, we treated a long line of patients who arrived on foot, on horseback and on motorbike from the surrounding villages. For many, we were the only medical professionals they had ever seen. My pseudo professionalism melted when I heard their tragic stories. One afternoon, a young woman arrived with her sick infant after trekking nearly ten miles to reach us. She was not lactating effectively, and her child lay emaciated and dying. As I administered fluids to the baby, I was amazed by my ability to make a difference in their lives.

Although I did not choose to enroll in medical school immediately after college, my desire to work in public health has never waned during my subsequent decade of academic, professional, and volunteer experiences. Armed with a BA in Biology and a MS in Public Health Services, I have pursued many diverse experiences to improve the availability of health care services on a worldwide basis. Each activity has strengthened my conviction that I can make a meaningful contribution to people's lives on both the individual and societal level. Moreover, I am confident that my various experiences will help me to be a broader, more informed, and more sensitive physician.

At Georgetown University, where I have taught classes in Public Health Policy for the past six years, my interest in cross-cultural communication drew me to study the relationships among medicine, the law and politics. These variables play a key role in determining a nation's commitment to public service, particularly regarding women's health issues. My studies taught me that improved infrastructure and health education might have prevented many of the conditions that we had treated in Africa. I acted on my concerns by working with the U.S. State Department in Zambia and Ghana, where I gained firsthand insight into policy formation.

But I also acknowledged a profound limitation; to help people in a direct and tangible way, I need a medical degree. Without support at the international level, programs such as the one I championed in Zambia and Ghana will cease to exist. After medical school, I hope to become a voice of hope for underserved regions, whose people cannot survive without the intervention of quality medical care and education. This spring, I will return to Zambia with Hope 2012, which is an outreach group from Georgetown, to establish rural health clinics on the outskirts of Jutta. I see my three-month commitment as an opportunity to bring short-term care to an underserved area that deserves a voice in the fledgling African health care system.

After I complete my medical degree, I will continue to work for groups like Hope 2012, which are committed to developing viable health care policies in emerging areas. Fifteen years after my first memorable trip to Zambia, I am excited to finally fulfill my destiny by enrolling in medical school. The skills I have acquired through research, policy analysis, volunteer work and cross-cultural interaction will enable me to make a meaningful contribution to the communities I serve.

Our Assessment: This statement, although short, reveals the author's distinguished record as a public health advocate. She was a welcome addition to the program that admitted her, which specializes in this area.

Older Candidate – Software Development Experience

Life presents everyone with fascinating questions…What do you want to be when you grow up? What college will you attend? Will you marry me? Not everyone answers the same questions, or in the same order. Recently, I have found myself pondering - and answering - a persistent question: Are you sure that you want to become a doctor?

My family, friends, and colleagues all remember the hectic schedule that my brother endured to graduate from medical school. At this point in my life, they wonder if I am ready to embrace such a grueling endeavor. Sadly, they have not considered the lingering questions that have fueled this professional decision. Am I fulfilled by my career as a software developer? Do I want to continue on the same path? After careful introspection, I have concluded that the answer is no.

As I progressed in my career at Facebook, I gained a wealth of practical skills. Initially, I thought that they only applied to computer engineering. Recently, I have concluded that the strengths that make me an excellent software developer are also essential in medicine. By listening to a customer's problem - and finding a solution - I have perfected my "diagnostic" skills. I have also learned to listen actively – and ask probing questions - to correctly assess my client's needs.

In engineering school - and throughout my career - I learned to think methodically and view scenarios from non-traditional perspectives. I also learned to act quickly in high pressure situations. On one occasion, I had to deliver a solution with zero fault tolerance. If the customer experienced an outage, we would incur millions of dollars in penalties. By working closely with my team - and establishing a clear set of expectations - we achieved this ambitious objective.

By leading cross-functional teams, I have also honed my interpersonal skills. During one of my assignments, I re-designed the testing process for the new Facebook timeline. To do so, I established new relationships between our test group and the development teams in the US, China, and India. By working closely with all of the teams - and fully assessing their needs - I implemented a system that increased efficiency, reduced headcount, and achieved $2 million in annual cost savings. Most importantly, I enjoyed a rewarding multi-cultural experience that broadened my perspective of our business.

Despite these achievements, my enthusiasm for my work eventually started to wane. In my heart, I yearned to make a more meaningful contribution to the world around me. At that point in time, I accompanied my church group on a mission trip to Haiti, where I installed pumps for their drinking water and volunteered at a clinic that served a rural population. By assisting the doctors - and seeing the patients' heartfelt gratitude for our help, I gained a renewed appreciation for the interpersonal aspects of medicine. I confirmed my desire to pursue a career that was more focused on people - and compassion – than the bottom line.

Upon my return to California, I began to consider the realities of becoming a physician, which requires years of study, training, and sacrifice. Yet it also offers a rare opportunity to think critically and continue learning, which is extremely important to me. On several occasions, I have discussed my intentions with my brother and his colleagues, who have graduated from medical school and embarked on challenging residencies. Their stories of loss and despair have deeply touched my heart.

Throughout our conversations, one question continually arose. Why would I pursue a career that brings sadness and grief? After careful reflection, I have concluded that this mixture of joy and sorrow is what makes the profession rewarding. I cannot cure every disease or save every patient, but I can certainly make a difference.

Throughout my life, I have learned many important lessons by asking - and answering - tough questions. My willingness to explore new ideas and opportunities has prepared me to accept the daunting responsibilities ahead. It has also given me the confidence and determination to choose a difficult path that most would never consider. As I prepare for a career in medicine, I am eager to explore wherever the journey may lead.

<u>Our Assessment</u>: This is an honest and insightful statement from a candidate who understood the implications of changing careers at 35. His strong science background, top MCAT score, and persuasive recommendation letters made a positive impression on the admissions committee.

Older Applicant – Teaching Experience

In high school, my mother affectionately called me her "rebel without a clue." As the daughter of two physicians, I resisted the automatic assumption that I was destined to follow in their footsteps. Nevertheless, I enjoyed our evening discussions about my father's cancer patients and the novel way he treated their diseases. My mother, a busy obstetrician, shared happier stories about the chubby babies she delivered in the middle of the night. Although I wasn't ready to commit to a medical career, I always felt a natural affinity for the field. I also understood that good health was not simply a blessing, but a miracle.

As a college student, I completed the prerequisites for medical school as part of my degree in secondary education. Rather than become a doctor, however, I opted to teach science classes at a newly formed magnet school in Atlanta. Being an educator in such a nurturing environment has been a very positive experience. During my first year, I established a formal tutoring program for the accelerated chemistry course. Remembering my own experiences in a lab environment, I could relate to the students' frustration about the lack of after-school support. Every Wednesday, I held support session to review their laboratory procedures, reports and problem sets. To my delight, three of my students subsequently obtained top scores on their SAT-II tests in Chemistry, which earned them advanced college credits. More importantly, they came to truly love the subject matter, which inspired their passion for learning.

After two years, I advanced to the role of Department Head in Biological Sciences at the Davis School. In this role, I supervise five teachers and three lab assistants who teach twelve separate laboratory courses. I also continue to deliver the lecture portion of the accelerated chemistry course, which attracts some of the brightest students in the district. From these experiences, I have learned how to communicate effectively to large groups of people. I have also learned how to create an environment that encourages questions and discussions. My relationships with my students have always been the most gratifying aspect of my job.

My gravitation to a medical career began on my first summer break, when I accepted a volunteer position in the Emergency Room at St. Mary's Hospital. Although I originally planned to provide computer support, I found myself captivated by the different cases I observed in the ER. Soon, I volunteered for additional responsibilities, including running simple lab tests and conducting intake interviews. Drawing upon my knowledge of medicine, I easily engaged the patients in discussions and seemed to have a soothing effect on them. I remembered my father's admonition that "an ounce of compassion was worth a pound of cure." Strangely, magnetically, as the summer wore on, my time at the hospital became the most enjoyable aspect of my life. I returned to my teaching job in the fall of 2004 with a plan to transition into medicine.

At first, I hesitated to tell my parents about my plan, for fear of hearing the inevitable "we told you so." To my surprise, they reacted to my news with a series of questions designed to flush out my underlying motivation. Knowing the strain of the profession, my parents wanted to make sure that I was entering the field for the right reasons, with the right set of expectations. I valued their perspective, along with their concern for my future. I also admire their respect for the medical profession and what it requires of those who choose it.

After succeeding as a teacher and mentor, my clinical experience was the "missing piece" of my preparation for medical school. Once I experienced the joy of helping patients in their time of need, I knew that I would never be equally satisfied in any other type of work. With my background as a teacher and researcher, I also hope to contribute to the advancement of medical science. By applying to medical school, I am taking my life in an exciting new direction that offers the capacity for great challenges and equally great satisfaction. After several years on an alternative path, I have finally decided what I want to do and who I want to be. Medicine is my destiny.

<u>Our Assessment</u>: This candidate was a distinguished teacher who had won several awards for her performance in the classroom. In this essay, she explains her circuitous route to medical school, including her early exposure to the field. The committee was impressed by the candidate's determination to follow her own path, rather than that of her parents. Her application was well perceived.

Older Applicants – Journalism Experience

As I began my watch, the Southern Cross hung low on the horizon. Suddenly, a dramatic squall transformed the quiet deck into an organized frenzy of activity that threatened our deep-water sampling program. My watch mates and I moved quickly, closing up hatches and hauling the scientific equipment aboard. Within minutes the stars disappeared, the gusts became violent, and a black wall of rain enveloped us. Although the elements were capricious, our carefully choreographed teamwork saved the day.

At the time, I was a 19-year-old deckhand aboard a research vessel run by the San Diego Sea Education Association (SDSEA), which was completing a three-month passage across the Atlantic. Most of us were freshmen or sophomores in college - old enough to fulfill the mission, but blissfully unaware of how it would change us. Lured by the romantic notion of pirates and buried treasure, we found ourselves learning the most unglamorous lessons in teamwork. By the time the storm hit us, we had evolved from a group of 20 individuals into a carefully coordinated team that worked hard together to keep our ship afloat. The grueling workload left little room for selfishness or goofing off. Ironically, for the first time in my life, I felt completely engaged.

Like a physician working on call, I rose to the demands of a punishing schedule, including significant mental and physical fatigue, amid the necessity of the work at hand. Life at sea was full of challenges that required me to exercise my mind, muscle and judgment to keep our vessel safely on her way. In the 15 years since I sailed for SDSEA, I have intentionally sought out academic and professional endeavors that were similarly intense and challenging.

Both at sea and on land, I have found great pleasure in the rewards of hard work and teamwork. After completing my degree in journalism at Stanford University, I embarked on a career as an editor for *San Diego Magazine*. Editing articles and news releases was a delicate project that required tact, good judgment and consensus building among a talented team of reporters, writers and interviewers. For each piece, we did our best to strike the proper balance between our readers' tastes and those of our administrators. Far too often, I found myself the reluctant leader who championed an unpopular (yet ethical) position that no one else had the courage to promote. Over time, my passion for writing and my reliable attitude enabled me to advance to the position of Editor-in-Chief at the magazine.

Despite my success as a journalist, my decision to become a physician has been brewing for several years. While receiving treatment for a chronic knee injury, I watched the doctors at San Diego General Hospital assuage the fear of a frightened five-year-old who needed to have her hand stitched. Immediately I recognized the value of the doctor's role as a healer. Likewise, when the orthopedic surgeon operated on my knee, I was impressed by the precision in the surgical ward, where each person performed his or her function in the fastest and most efficient manner. Just like the crew members on our research ship, they were part of a finely-tuned machine.

Before I completed my medical school applications, I confirmed my interest by volunteering in two contrasting medical settings: a low-income neighborhood clinic and the emergency room of a private pediatric hospital. As I worked with patients and experienced the daily challenges of a practitioner, I was drawn to the powerful effect of the physician-patient relationship. Eventually, I hope to become a physician of the highest caliber who can inspire a similar level of trust in my own patients.

The common thread in my diverse achievements is my love of intellectual challenge and rigor. After using these skills as an editor, I am eager to re-direct my energy in a more humanitarian context. Medicine is a perfect way to merge my skills and interests; I can bring everything I have (analytical reasoning, social conscience, compassion, a sense of teamwork) into the arena. Although the road ahead is a humbling one, I am eager to embark on it. By becoming a physician, I can do more than simply fulfill my own desires; I can make a lasting contribution to a deserving community.

Our Assessment: As a seasoned journalist, this author gave the reader a dramatic opening that immediately captured their interest. Then, he artfully told the story of his career trajectory, which ultimately led him to medical school. There are several artful transitions in this statement that allowed the author to cover several topics in a relatively short space. The resulting statement was well perceived.

Older Candidate: Writer

Three years ago, a frightful brush with a libel suit rekindled my long-dormant desire to be a physician. As the Lifestyle Editor of the *Kansas City Star*, I wrote a headline story about a local woman who had died of a heart attack after taking phen-fen, the deadly diet drug combination of fenfluramine and phentermine. As news of additional phen-fen related deaths assaulted the media, I investigated how the drug works and the abbreviated approval process the Food & Drug Administration (FDA) had used to rush it to the marketplace. The feedback from our readership was overwhelmingly positive.

A few weeks later, my Editor-in-Chief called me into his office and told me that American Home Products, which is the drug company that manufactured and marketed phen-fen, was suing the newspaper over the story and had specifically cited the headline, which characterized the drug as "reckless." He and the executive editor assured me the coverage and headline were fair. Even so, I began to fear for my job.

Sensing my concern, the managing editor had me meet with the newspaper's medical consultant, who shared my boss's confidence. The consultant was reassuring and, as I realized later, inspiring, as he discussed the need for newspapers and magazines to publish accurate information about the health implications of so-called "miracle drugs." This experience taught me more than the importance of careful word choice; it reminded me of how closely I had come to following an alternative career path in the medical field.

Twelve years earlier, I decided to major in journalism as a college freshman. My choice was not necessarily my "calling," but my desire to impress my father, who had enjoyed a wildly successful career in the same profession. Although I felt drawn to a career in medicine, I lacked the courage to stand up for my own convictions. Fortunately, I had a gift for writing and speaking, which translated into good grades in my journalism classes at Stanford. Nevertheless, in my heart, the "fit" was never quite right. From the start, I only felt energized when I reported on health-related stories. During my senior year at Stanford, I served as the Nutrition Editor of the campus newspaper, which required me to evaluate the plethora of fad diets that pervaded the campus. I also indulged my passion for medicine by completing several related courses in biology, nutrition and exercise science. For the first time, I discovered the joy of pursuing my own interests.

After graduation, I accepted a less prestigious position as a writer for the *Kansas City Star* because it allowed me to report on the "softer" type of medical stories that I had come to enjoy. My father's disappointment paled in comparison to the fulfillment I received from my job. Every story gave me the chance to research and report another aspect of human health. Eventually, my passion paid off. In 2005, after I published a twelve-part expose on the unreported medical risks associated with saline breast implants, I earned a Peabody Award for excellence in investigative reporting.

Occasionally, when I interviewed doctors, I felt a twinge of envy that I was not part of their profession. The feeling was particularly acute when I met with the medical consultant about phen-fen, who assured me that my story was neither reckless nor libelous. In a rare moment of candor, I told him that I had always wanted to become a physician. When he asked what was stopping me, I couldn't think of a single intelligent response.

Fortunately, my anxiety over the suit was brief. The newspaper quickly prevailed, and I remained a valued editor, although my priorities had clearly changed. I was no longer content to watch from the sidelines while physicians waged the real health care battles. The final epiphany from the lawsuit gave me the push I needed to change the direction of my life. While still working for the newspaper, I quietly began the application process for medical school.

Six months after the libel suit, my best friend gave birth to a baby girl. During this time of happiness and introspection, I wondered what wisdom I could possibly impart to her. It was actually quite simple: don't be afraid to follow your heart. By finally pursing a medical career, I am taking my own advice.

Our Assessment: This candidate was always drawn to medicine, but she followed an alternative path after college in order to please her father. In this statement, she eloquently explains what motivated her to resume her original plans. On a competitive basis, the essay was risky, because it did not discuss the author's volunteer work in clinical settings, which allowed her to confirm her career change. Thankfully, she submitted an excellent recommendation letter from an MD who confirmed her work at a local hospital.

Older Applicants

When I enrolled at Princeton in 2002, I was amazed by the number of students who were already classified as "premed." I wondered how they were able to decide with such certainty that they wanted to study medicine, without taking the time to explore other professional opportunities. Despite my proclivity for the sciences, I was reluctant to commit myself to a particular career at eighteen. After all, what if my true calling was psychology, or marketing or teaching? How could I close the door on so many possibilities that I hadn't even begun to explore?

Unlike the "early committers," I viewed my college years as an opportunity for personal growth and exploration. One of my greatest adventures came at the end of my sophomore year, when I accepted a volunteer position at an orphanage in Brazil. For the entire summer, I lived with twenty young girls and four Portuguese-speaking nuns in a village outside Salvador. My daily chores included caring for the babies and teaching the older girls to speak English. Since the orphanage was always shorthanded, I also harvested vegetable crops before they were destroyed by the summer floods; I even raised chickens to add an extra protein source to our diets.

Although I enjoyed working with the children, I regretted that I did not have any specific skill or service to offer them. I particularly wished that I could provide a reliable source of health care, which was always in short supply. When I returned to Princeton in the fall of 2004, the thought of becoming a doctor continued to be an intriguing possibility. Unfortunately, my coursework as a Finance major meant that changing course would require me to complete several years of pre-medical prerequisites. For a scholarship student with minimal resources, it was the wrong time to change direction.

After graduation, I enjoyed a rapid series of promotions in my career as a financial analyst for Bear Stearns, yet I missed the sense of satisfaction that I had experienced while working with the children in Brazil. Through judicious use of the company's tuition reimbursement program, I slowly and methodically completed the science and math classes that were required to achieve a top score on the MCAT. Thankfully, my success in the business world also changed my perspective about the sacrifices required to prepare for a medical career. In college, the idea of completing four years of medical school, followed by another four or five years in a residency program, seemed overwhelming. Five years later, the tradeoff seemed quite reasonable for the skills that I would acquire. I was finally ready, on a psychological, financial and educational basis, to embrace the challenges that would accompany the pursuit of such an intellectually stimulating profession.

For the past two years, in addition to my work at Bear Stearns, I have volunteered as an intake officer at Mercy Hospital in Brooklyn. In this capacity, I interview each patient before (s)he is seen by a doctor, at which time I record each patient's history, symptoms and vital signs. After several weeks on the job, I gained confidence in my ability to put patients at ease and ask pertinent questions. Last month, I advanced to a position in the medical lab, where I conduct routine tests and deliver specimens to various departments. Through this work, I have gained an understanding of how the hospital functions as a synchronized unit to deliver efficient and compassionate care.

Through these diverse experiences, I have confirmed my longstanding suspicion that I was meant to become a physician. Although the seed was not planted during childhood, it has certainly survived and taken root over the past ten years. By taking pre-medical courses, volunteering at Mercy Hospital and getting to know other non-traditional pre-medical students, I have discovered that an early interest in medicine is not necessarily a prerequisite to success. Some of us benefit from taking time after college to reach that conclusion, after we have explored other options. By doing so, I have developed a wealth of skills that I will bring to medical school, along with a mature understanding of my goals and motivation. I am eager to share all of my blessings with my future peers at Harvard Medical School.

Our Assessment: In this statement, the candidate answered the questions that haunt many older applicants and career changers: why medicine? Why now? And why didn't you choose it in the first place? Her explanations were simple, honest, and straightforward. They also show the considerable time and energy she invested to turn this dream into reality.

Older Applicant – Professor of Women's Studies

Emotional. Overbearing. Unable to accept criticism. At first, the women winced when they heard the negative adjectives ascribed to them by their male colleagues. Eventually, as the second-hand comments became less rational and more ridiculous, the discussion evolved into a raucous laughter borne of their collective pain.

Sadly, the women at the meeting were not office workers or waitresses at a local coffee shop. They were practicing physicians who were respected members of the British Medical Women's Association (BMWA). As the corresponding secretary of the group, I was responsible for moderating the discussion about sexual inequities in the work place. For most, the experience was cathartic. By sharing their private pain, the participants realized that they were not the only ones who endured such shabby and unnecessary treatment.

As a Professor of Women's Studies at the American University in London, I have devoted my entire career to the promotion of gender equality. A committed feminist, I have published numerous articles about women's issues, along with a comprehensive report on the past, the present and the future of British women doctors. My affiliation with the BMWA evolved from our shared desire to raise awareness about controversial social and political causes. The medical profession, particularly in academia, is usually too conservative to encourage open discourse on difficult subjects. Despite the pressure to remain silent, BMWA members are no longer afraid to vocalize their beliefs. I am honored to be their official voice to the media.

In my five years as the corresponding secretary for the group, we have lobbied tirelessly for equal employment opportunities. Whenever possible, we raise awareness about blatant inequalities that female physicians encounter in the workplace. In 2004, I was invited to present the keynote speech to the British Medical Association, which was attended by Prime Minister Tony Blair. His thoughtful questions and comments encouraged many BMWA members to pursue ambitious and non-traditional career paths. The Prime Minister's verbal support was a much-needed boost to our idealism and tenacity.

For many years, I have yearned to play a more direct and meaningful role in educating and protecting women. During this time, I have watched in silence as women have been victimized by sexual abuse and domestic violence. Sadly, even in life-threatening situations, many women are too intimidated to report this violence or fight for their legal rights; I admire the BMWA's efforts to bring attention to such important matters. By creating and promoting awareness programs on various social issues, they have helped to protect and improve the lives of countless women and children.

Ultimately, they have also inspired me to re-claim my long-lost dream of becoming a physician. When I first considered the possibility two or three years ago, I wondered if I had waited too long to seize the opportunity. At 35, was it too late to go to medical school? According to my good friend Dr. Sheila Myers-Kynd, the answer is an emphatic "no!"

Although age has given me gray hair and the occasional wrinkle, it has also given me a wealth of practical experience in all aspects of sociology and human behavior. In addition to my academic training, I also have extensive experience as a writer, speaker, teacher and advocate. Throughout my time at American University, I have been the catalyst for many thought-provoking discussions about medical, social and political issues, for which I have offered a female perspective. Who better to sit in a medical school classroom?

On a personal level, I am 100% prepared to make the necessary sacrifices to change careers. From my work with the BMWA, I know the challenges that women face to succeed, both in the medical profession and in society. I am confident that I will not only be a compassionate physician, but a voice for social change. With the exceptional training I will receive at Harvard Medical School, I hope to embody the best that the medical profession has to offer.

Our Assessment: This candidate was already well-recognized in medical circles for her work as an advocate. In this statement, which is honest, concise, and logically written, she explains her motivation for enrolling in medical school. On a technical basis, there are gaps – she does not explore her science background or clinical experiences, which were particularly impressive. Thankfully, the author's transcripts and recommendation letters confirmed that she was an intelligent and driven person who possessed the requisite stamina to complete a medical degree. She was a tremendous asset to the program she joined.

Older Candidate - Scholarship Request (Based on Financial Need)

According to philosophers, a smart man knows when to ask for help – and is not afraid to do so. He also knows that his greatest goals in life will require tremendous dedication and sacrifice, regardless of the help that he receives. As I embark on the path to medical school, I am proud of the achievements – and sacrifices – that I have made on my professional journey. Through hard work and dedication, I published three articles on HIV transmission while working full-time at an AIDS hospice. I also earned a 34 on my MCAT while obtaining top grades in a Ph.D. program at UCLA. By obtaining a solid background in science, along with practical experience in a clinical setting, I have confirmed my suitability and passion for this rigorous field.

Nevertheless, as a self-supporting student with little savings, I will face a formidable challenge to finance my medical school education. I also face the additional hurdle of paying off $60,000 in outstanding student loan debt, which I incurred during my MS and Ph.D. programs in Public Health. Despite these obstacles, I am determined to complete my medical degree and embark on a career in epidemiology, which will enable me to make a lasting difference in people's lives. However, I will require financial assistance to bring this dream to fruition.

Based on my financial limitations, I believe that I will qualify for a needs-based scholarship from your organization; hopefully, my achievements as a student, researcher, and public health specialist will also make me an attractive candidate for merit-based awards. At this stage in the admissions process, I am eager to be considered for both types of scholarships.

Throughout my Ph.D. program, I have spoken to several physicians about their medical school experiences. As a result, I am well aware of the crippling nature of student loan payments, which will impact my eventual ability to buy a house, support my family, and pursue a lower-paying specialty. As part of my preparation for medical school, I am exploring every possible way to minimize my long-term debt and keep my focus on my education.

At 35, I will bring a mature perspective to my studies, along with significant practical experience. After years of preparation, I am ready to embrace the personal, academic, and clinical challenges that medical school will bring. At my recent campus visit, I spoke to several prospective students about the possibility of forming study groups to boost morale and improve our academic performance. I am eager to take an active role in my education and to help others to do the same.

With scholarship assistance from your organization, I will have the opportunity to achieve my academic goals and make a tangible contribution to the student body. After graduation, I will fulfill a lifelong dream that offers long-term benefits to my family, peers, and the patients who will rely upon me.

Our Assessment: Unfortunately, there are few scholarships for medical school students, who must borrow a significant amount of money in order to complete their education. This candidate won several need-based awards with this essay, which presented his strengths in an honest and straightforward manner.

Older Candidate from Disadvantaged Neighborhood

In my impoverished neighborhood in south Chicago, few of my friends escaped the temptation of drugs, crime, and violence. The proliferation of gangs – and the lack of positive role models – made education a low priority. By the time I was a teenager, I knew that I wanted a better future - and that I would do whatever was necessary to create it. In a world of followers and despair, I was determined to become a leader.

In difficult times, my mother provided a powerful source of direction. Without a spouse or education, she worked long hours in a low paying job simply to make ends meet. Nevertheless, my mother never regretted making this sacrifice on my behalf. Her fondest wish was for me to graduate from college and pursue a rewarding career, which she never had the chance to do. An education, she insisted, would open the door to a lifetime of opportunities.

At age 10, I found salvation in an unlikely place – the world of Kajukenbo. Through focus and dedication, I mastered this amazing martial art, which combines unique aspects of judo, boxing, karate, and kung fu. At first, when I began to learn Kajukenbo, I was simply exploring an athletic passion; I did not realize the many ways that it would change my life. Over time, the hours of practice and conditioning gave me a sense of maturity that few of my peers possessed. I gained the confidence to join the math team, the cross country team, and to excel in my high school classes. Eventually, I decided to share my expertise in martial arts by teaching Kajukenbo to the children in my neighborhood. I was eager to give them a positive alternative to the crime and violence on our streets.

In 2006, I fulfilled my mother's greatest dream when I graduated from high school and enrolled in the Physical Therapy program at the University of Florida. After years of competitive training, I wanted to learn as much as possible about the human body. In the classroom, I completed a rigorous academic program, including advanced courses in anatomy and physiology. I also earned a silver medal at the Martial Arts Olympics, which attracted seasoned competitors from across the globe. My successful performance at this event cemented my position as a role model in my community. By sharing my expertise in Kajukenbo, I acknowledged my ability – and desire - to help people improve their lives.

With this in mind, I joined the volunteer program at Gainesville Memorial Hospital, where I completed my rotations for my Physical Therapy degree. Immediately, I saw the impact of poverty, ignorance, and fear. Far too often, our patients did not seek medical assistance until their conditions were fairly serious – and significantly harder to cure. Whenever possible, I used my skills as a communicator to explain the importance of positive lifestyle choices, such as diet, exercise, and proper hygiene, and regular screenings for diabetes, cancer, and heart disease. Sadly, in most cases, the patients' family practitioners had failed to convey this essential information.

When I worked with patients – and learned more about their conditions – I found myself deeply invested in their needs. I was humbled by the chance to play a meaningful role in their recoveries. On several occasions, I suggested alternative therapies that might help them, such as acupuncture and chiropractic techniques. Other times, I simply provided a compassionate ear during a difficult time. More than anything, I wanted the chance to earn the trust that my patients had placed in me.

By working in clinical settings, I have confirmed my ability to succeed in this fast-paced environment. I have also gained an appreciation for the practical aspects of medicine, including the need to deliver quality care to a heterogeneous population. Physicians will face numerous challenges in the next few years, including the high cost of care, which prevents the poorest and sickest patients from seeking timely intervention. There are also continual frustrations relating to insurance, bureaucracy, and patient noncompliance. Nevertheless, medicine also offers exciting new developments, such as the discovery of genetic networks that provide considerable insight into the disease process. Looking ahead, I cannot imagine a more satisfying future than finding creative solutions to these challenges.

Throughout my life, I have worked diligently to escape the crime and poverty that permeate my neighborhood. By doing so, I have acquired the skills that I will need to help others do the same. Looking back, my greatest achievements are not my diplomas or medals; they are the moments when I enhanced someone's life as a teacher, physical therapist, and role model. After medical school, I hope to serve society in a more tangible way, by finding better ways to treat, diagnose, and prevent human disease.

I am particularly eager to practice in an underserved area, where I can implement viable programs in health education and preventive medicine. With my background in physical therapy and my passion to serve others, I can catalyze change in these communities – and in the lives of the patients who rely upon me. By doing so, I will provide a ray of hope to people like my mother, who deserve the best that medicine has to offer.

Our Assessment: This candidate grew up in a poor neighborhood were few students graduated from high school. His considerable success, which he attributes primarily to his mother's support and his martial arts training, was deeply inspirational to the admissions committee. As an added bonus, the candidate had impeccable credentials as a physical therapist, which added diversity to the medical school class.

Older Candidate Applying for a Dual Ph.D. Program

On a philosophical level, knowledge is the greatest treasure on earth. Money, power, fame - all pale in comparison to the power of knowledge. As a student, I have devoted my life to learning as much as possible about the world so that I can help to improve it. As a teacher, I have assumed the awesome responsibility of empowering others to do the same. My motivation to complete my MD and PhD at Brown is to prepare for a career in medical education, to devote my life to the dissemination of knowledge.

I love teaching. Beginning in junior high school, I tutored my peers in subjects as diverse as math, biology, chemistry, physics and statistics. Later, in college, I worked as a part-time tutor to defray my educational expenses. Immediately after my graduation from Temple University, I began a rewarding five-year teaching career in the Junction City school system in rural Kansas. By gaining experience in such diverse social, geographical and cultural environments, I have confirmed the power of education to open both minds and hearts.

Teaching has also enabled me to critically evaluate my own skills. With every theory I explain, I better understand my own thought processes. On a philosophical level, every experiment I lead in my science classes releases a fresh light into the traditional room of thought. Likewise, every question I answer reveals a new perspective of both conventional views and more orthodox methods. To teach is also to learn.

When I teach, I see myself in the student that sits across from me; I recall the same confusion that I experienced when I was learning the same material. Likewise, when I see the look of comprehension in the eyes of a student, I experience a profound sense of satisfaction. By passing on the knowledge that my teachers once imparted to me, I have re-paid a cosmic debt and advanced my own mind in the process. As a teacher, I am part of a rewarding cycle of giving and learning more about myself on a daily basis.

Thankfully, education provides a rewarding type of karma; the more knowledge I possess, the more I can enlighten others. At first, I struggled with the decision to acquire an MD or a PhD. Although I am drawn to the challenges of patient care, I simply cannot abandon my call to be an educator. A dual degree program is the logical choice for my particular goals. The MD program will train me in the clinical side of medicine, while the PhD program will provide the requisite science background I will need to teach at the university level. Completing both degrees at Brown will provide an extraordinary opportunity to master both the practical and didactic aspects of medicine in a community of top-level educators and practitioners. Consequently, I am applying for admission to the joint MD/PhD program at Brown University Medical School. As an educator, I am eager to do my part to acquire and spread medical knowledge to make the world a safer and healthier place in which to live.

Our Assessment: This candidate had already been accepted to the MD program before he applied for admission to the PhD program at the same school. In this statement, he explains his reason for completing a dual degree; eventually, he hopes to use his skills as a teacher at the university level.

Chapter 6: Secondary Essays

In addition to reviewing their primary statements, many medical schools ask candidates to discuss an ethical dilemma, a personal weakness, or how they will contribute to the diversity on campus. Other schools ask candidates to describe their future in 10 years – do they want to teach, conduct research, or run their own practice? If you are asked to answer these secondary essay questions, you must provide a response that is focused, detailed, and persuasive, regardless of the length limit. Ideally, the information you present should complement – rather than duplicate – the material in your other essays for that school.

As always, the power is in the details. For the diversity question, you should tell your life story in a creative and entertaining way. Bear in mind, diversity encompasses far more than just race; it also refers to your interests, talents, upbringing, religion, hobbies, family size, hometown, travel experiences, and socioeconomic standing. No two candidates have had the same life experiences, which is what makes this question interesting. If written honestly and openly, this essay can reveal a lot about who you are, what you value, and who you eventually hope to be.

The following essays vary widely in length and topic, but they all handled secondary essay topics in an extraordinary way. By design, we have organized the essays in the following sub-categories:

An Ethical Dilemma
Discuss a Personal Weakness
How You Will Contribute to the School's Diversity
A Significant Clinical, Research, or Volunteer Experience
Describe Your Future Practice

To protect the privacy of the writer, the names of all people, classes, schools, places, teams, activities, and companies have been changed.

Discuss a Personal, Ethical, or Academic Problem

As an ICU nurse at the University of San Francisco Medical Center, I work with patients of all racial, cultural and ethnic backgrounds. Occasionally, my own status as a Chinese-American creates a complex issue relating to medical ethics. One case last November was particularly challenging. An elderly Chinese woman who was diagnosed with terminal cancer had only a short time to live. According to contemporary ethics in Western medicine, the doctors were required to disclose her condition and offer all available treatment options. Unfortunately, her family vehemently opposed this disclosure. Because the woman's death was imminent, they felt that any discussion regarding her prognosis would be impossibly cruel.

As someone who was raised in China and educated in the United States, I understood both positions. In China, the family's wish would have superseded the medical community's desire for full disclosure. The patient would have been allowed to live out her final days in comfort and peace. In America, however, the medical community is compelled to offer all available treatments, even in terminal cases. They will not promote ignorance or encourage false hope. The American perspective also acknowledges the need for the family to resolve legal issues, such as the execution of a living will. Sharing the prognosis in a timely manner gives the patient time to plan the funeral and make appropriate arrangements to settle the estate.

In this particular case, a higher power resolved the situation for us, as the patient died before the doctors could disclose her prognosis. Under the circumstances, it was the best possible ending. Despite our best efforts to provide quality care to all patients, cultural clashes and ethical dilemmas are fairly common in multicultural health care settings. Families and physicians must work together on a case-by-case basis to find mutually-agreeable solutions.

<u>Our Assessment</u>: By choosing this topic, the candidate had a unique opportunity to showcase her maturity, professional skills, and multicultural perspective. In a short space, she gave a great analysis of an extremely complex issue.

Discuss a Personal, Ethical, or Academic Problem

During my junior year at UCLA, I roomed with a friend I had known since grade school. At the beginning of our second semester, Justin began to exhibit erratic behavior. Every weekend, he drank excessively and did not return until the next morning. On several occasions, Justin bragged about his activities, which included the use of alcohol and illegal drugs. Not surprisingly, as his grades began to slip, Justin became increasingly withdrawn from his family and friends.

At first, I felt powerless to help him. Finally, after Justin was arrested for possession of cannabis, I refused to remain silent. With the support of two friends on the soccer team, I staged an intervention in our dorm room, where we confronted Justin about his self-destructive behavior. One by one, we expressed our concern for his welfare and our willingness to help him recover.

Unfortunately, Justin resented our efforts and refused to acknowledge his problem. In subsequent weeks, he continued to withdraw from us and to drink excessively. Eventually, he flunked out of UCLA and accepted a job at a fast food restaurant in our hometown. Our friendship, which had literally begun in the sandbox, was permanently damaged.

This experience gave me painful insight into the power of addiction. On a personal basis, it confirmed my decision to abstain from drinking and drugs. On a professional basis, it demonstrated what I will encounter as a physician, when patients ignore my advice in favor of self-destructive habits. Despite the frustration and disappointment, I will continue to try to help them.

Our Assessment: The ethical dilemma question is hard for most candidates, because they must choose a topic in which they honored their conscience and made the "correct" choice. Sometimes, those situations are too difficult or personal to talk about. Other times, the word limit is too short to really tell the story effectively. This author presented his dilemma in an effective way without exceeding the length limit. Although he and Justin did not enjoy a happy ending, the candidate made a genuine effort to help his friend turn his life around. The rest was beyond his control.

Discuss a Personal, Ethical, or Academic Problem

At age six, I discovered that I was adopted. I also learned that I was a welcome gift to my loving parents, who had waited for several years to receive a healthy baby. Since then, I have always viewed adoption as a miraculous process that made the three of us a family.

In the same vein, I tend to have a negative view of abortion. At seventeen, I re-evaluated my perspective when my younger cousin unexpectedly became pregnant. To my surprise, she called me one evening and confided that she was thinking about having an abortion. My initial instinct was to tell her not to do it. However, I did not want to turn my cousin away when she desperately needed my acceptance and support.

During our conversation, I discovered the many factors that would influence her decision, including money, jobs, timing, and commitment. Although she loved her boyfriend, neither was prepared to raise and nurture a child. Finally, when I asked her about the possibility of adoption, my cousin quickly dismissed the idea. Once she saw the baby, she would never be able to give it away. My heart sank when I heard those words, because I knew that they were probably true.

In the end, I helped my cousin to evaluate the pros and cons of each option. When she asked my opinion, I told her that every choice had benefits and pitfalls. Although abortions are tragic, it is also tragic when children are abused by parents who are not ready or able to take care of them. Ultimately, she had to make the best decision on her own behalf, with no outside pressure.

This situation forced me to acknowledge my bias against abortion, which was stronger than I had imagined. Looking back, I am proud that I could set those feelings aside and offer unconditional support to my cousin. I also recognized that life presents everyone with situations that have no "easy" or obvious answers, because each alternative presents its own difficulties and tradeoffs. Rather than force my opinion on others, I will keep an open mind and allow them to make an informed choice that honors their individual needs. In return, I hope that they will offer me the same courtesy.

Our Assessment: This is a lovely essay on a highly controversial topic. The candidate handled it in a mature and loving way, without compromising her own feelings. She also provided unconditional support to her cousin during a difficult time, which was not the easiest thing to do. We have rarely seen this topic presented so honestly and objectively.

Describe a personal weakness and the steps you have taken to overcome it

When I was younger, I avoided conflict at all costs. Many times, I walked away from a potential argument, rather than defend my position and hold the other party accountable for his/her actions. Later, I would question whether I had sacrificed too much for the sake of keeping the peace.

Logically, I know that conflict is an inevitable part of life; I can't possibly please everyone all the time. As a physician, I must possess the confidence to express my opinions in a positive manner and to encourage others to do the same. Consequently, it was essential for me to develop this level of assertiveness in my personal and professional life.

A year ago, I took a communications course that required me to assess situations and defend my positions in class. Over time, I became much more comfortable expressing my opinions and supporting them with facts. Additionally, while reading my assignments for the course, I noted my feelings and developed my position before I attended class. By taking this step, I avoided the risk of being unduly influenced by other students, who expressed themselves more forcefully.

Finally, when I find myself in a contentious situation, I have learned to keep people's opinions in the proper perspective. Most of the time, they are not inherently right or wrong; they are simply someone's preference. I have also accepted that disagreements can be beneficial, if they encourage people to discuss all sides of an argument. For example, when I confronted a classmate who did not complete her portion of a group assignment, we developed a more trusting friendship. In fact, my teammates were grateful to me for insisting that we divide the workload equally. Thanks to these positive experiences, I now realize that I do not have to sacrifice my own thoughts and opinions just to keep the peace.

Our Assessment: This is a short but eloquent discussion of the candidate's shyness, which prevented her from confronting people and speaking up in class. By explaining the ways that she overcame this tendency and learned to assert herself, she made a positive impression on the reader.

Describe a personal weakness and the steps you have taken to overcome it

In high school and college, I prided myself on being an excellent student with a highly analytical nature. No class, regardless of its demands, was too tough for me to handle. Unfortunately, my ten-year gap between college and graduate school eroded my confidence in my academic potential. Although I was thrilled to complete my Master's degree at Stanford, I questioned my ability to succeed in such a rigorous and competitive academic environment.

During my first semester, I was sometimes intimidated by the talented professors and physicians who discussed their research projects at departmental meetings. Compared to me, they all seemed so focused and confident. As a result, I tended to remain quiet and second guess myself, rather than make suggestions. Not surprisingly, I rarely felt that I was working at my full potential as a student or researcher.

To conquer this self-doubt, I solicited a mentor who had significant experience in my intended area of research. With Daphne's support, I took an active role in the design of our study, which we presented to several planning and funding groups on campus. Over time, I learned to articulate my thoughts clearly and confidently about this important project, which offered tangible benefits to patients with Type II diabetes. By leading meetings and expressing my opinions, I have recognized my ability to contribute to the body of scientific knowledge at Stanford. Eventually, I hope to pay this kindness forward by playing the same role in other students' lives, to help them fulfill their highest potential.

Our Assessment: This candidate, who had an impressive track record as a researcher, also struggled to find his niche in a highly competitive graduate program. In this essay, he discusses this battle, which his mentor helped him to win. The candidate's recommendation letters confirmed his transformation into a strong and confident leader.

Describe a personal weakness and the steps you have taken to overcome it

My greatest weakness is self-criticism – I am rarely satisfied with the quality of my work. Even when my family, friends, and professors have assured me that a paper or project is exceptional, I will continue to try to improve it. In selecting classes and activities, I also tend to be somewhat conservative. Rather than risk personal embarrassment or a negative outcome, I make choices that are "safe" but sometimes unsatisfying.

Ironically, my perfectionism stem from the high expectations I have set for myself. Thankfully, I have acknowledged this weakness and am trying to be more flexible. Rather than catastrophize a situation, I step back and assess things objectively. By participating in social and athletic activities, I have become more comfortable in group situations and have opened my world to new experiences. I have particularly benefited from non-competitive activities, such as crafts and creative writing, which do not require me to "beat" another person. These enjoyable pursuits have taught me how to relax and have fun.

After careful introspection, I have realized that I cannot control every aspect of my life - sometimes things go wrong. By keeping a realistic perspective, I have balanced my desire for perfection with the knowledge that even the most talented and committed people sometimes make mistakes.

Our Assessment: This essay is strong, concise, and brutally honest. It was not easy for this candidate to admit how goal-oriented he was, which prevented him from enjoying his achievements. Although his "recovery" is definitely a work in progress, the committee was impressed by his honesty and insight on such a difficult topic.

Your Contribution to the Program's Diversity

After my father's death, my mother and I faced an unenviable challenge: to condense his 80 years on earth into a 50-word obituary. We quickly realized that we couldn't convey his achievements in 50 pages, much less 50 words. In Dad's case, the impact that he left, on both his family and community, defied conventional explanation.

Beginning at age 12, my father worked in the coal mines alongside his widowed father. Because he had to raise his brothers and sisters, Dad received little formal education, yet he eventually owned his own landscaping business. I always respected his adaptability and resourcefulness. Although he never had a lot of money, my father always made sure we had whatever we needed to succeed. My father particularly hoped that I would become the first person in the family to attend college. There's no doubt in my mind that he would be thrilled to know that I am applying to medical school.

Being "the first" member of my family to leave the nest has been a mixed blessing. On one hand, my family is extremely proud of every accomplishment, whether I make the dean's list or get an internship. Being the educational pioneer in the family, I have also never been pressured to follow someone else's path. On the down side, my entire educational career has been filled with unknowns. Although being a pioneer is exciting, it can also be scary and exhausting.

Since neither of my parents had attended college, they were unable to offer me much advice about the admissions process. As a result, I relied on my high school guidance counselor for the simplest things. While filling out the applications, I was a nervous wreck. I had never heard of a financial aid form, and I had certainly never written a personal statement. Throughout college, I had many intimidating "firsts." Away from my family for the first time, I constantly got lost on the crowded streets of Philadelphia. Once classes started, I felt alone at a very large school, so I decided to become involved in student organizations. By taking the initiative to make friends, my world expanded far beyond the borders of the tiny mining town in which I was raised.

My college graduation was bittersweet; to my family, it represented the culmination of a dream. A Conner child had actually graduated from college. For me, though, my father's absence was a painful reminder that the man who had enabled my success had not lived to see it. To this day, I gain considerable comfort from the knowledge that he is watching over me wherever I go. Although the challenges I face are nothing in comparison to his, I know he would be proud that I am going to be a doctor. After all, I am the one who took care of him throughout his three-year battle with cancer.

The most important thing I learned in college was to always push myself. If I had followed the easy road, I would never have accomplished what I have. I am grateful to my father for teaching me that and for giving me the courage to achieve more than what is expected.

Our Assessment: With no length restriction, this candidate had the luxury of writing a comprehensive statement that revealed the many challenges she faced, including her father's death, her rural upbringing, and her struggle to adapt to college life. Combined with her primary statement, which discussed her work in public health, she gave the committee a balanced view of her credentials.

Your Contribution to the Program's Diversity

"Buenos Dias! Cómo se siente usted?" As a child, I was enthralled by my Spanish classes. When I looked at the globe, I was enticed by the idea of visiting places in which this romantic language was spoken. With this in mind, I embarked on numerous excursions to improve my oral and written fluency. Some of my experiences were intellectual, such as my language classes at the University of Barcelona. Others were recreational, such as my month-long vacation in Madrid and Seville. But none was more challenging – or satisfying – than working at a children's free clinic in Belize.

Every day, I assisted the physicians at this busy facility, which served the needs of immigrant families that did not have access to health care. Not surprisingly, my language skills were immediately put to good use. Before the trip, I wondered if my natural shyness would impede my ability to communicate. Thankfully, in the presence of our grateful patients, my confidence immediately blossomed.

My work at the clinic provided a stimulating way for me to hone my skills as a caregiver. I have rarely had the opportunity to learn, feel, or experience so much. The poverty in the region – and the need for preventive health care – highlighted my passion to make a difference. When I returned to Wyoming, I made immediate plans to return to Belize during the summer of 2011. I am eager to make similar trips – and professional contributions – throughout my medical career.

Our Assessment: This candidate provided a charming and informative answer in an extremely short space. As an added bonus, she mentioned her volunteer work in Belize, which she did not have room to include in her primary statement.

Your Contribution to the Program's Diversity

As a child, I was deeply influenced by my father's Iranian culture, which inspired my love of ancient poetry and my respect for old age and wisdom. At the same time, my upbringing in the United States encouraged me to approach life in a practical manner, with an eye towards my professional future. These two perspectives, although different, gave me a profound sense of optimism and dignity. Each year, my family celebrates the Persian New Year, which signifies the first day of spring. By honoring the rebirth of nature, we express our hope that the New Year will bring happiness and prosperity. Likewise, we also celebrate the Western New Year, which honors the same ideals with different traditions and festivities.

As a first generation Iranian-American, I will bring a strong appreciation for different cultures to my medical career. I will also bring my awareness of the psychological and social influences on human behavior. By acknowledging people's unique needs and expectations, I can develop more trusting relationships with my peers, patients and their families. I can also deliver culturally sensitive care to patients whose backgrounds and customs are very different from my own.

Finally, my graduate studies in public health have broadened my knowledge of health care and provided a realistic perspective of the challenges doctors face on a daily basis. I am eager to solve contemporary problems in medicine, including the lack of quality care for society's poorest and sickest members. By approaching these issues with a strong mind and an open heart, I can help to promote the health of others, which will build a stronger and more cohesive society.

Our Assessment: In a short space, this candidate gave the reader a unique view of his cultural background and graduate training in public health, which would allow him to make a distinctive contribution to his medical school class.

Your Contribution to the Program's Diversity

Every day, after the final bell at school, I ran to the convenience store in downtown Cicero that my parents owned and operated. Between four and midnight, I served a steady stream of customers who bought gas, snack food, and lottery tickets on their way home from work. To my younger siblings, this was a thankless job with few intrinsic rewards. Yet, to me, our successful business was proof of our family's ability to build a successful life in America. By working hard and watching our finances, my parents managed to purchase a home, launch their business, and support our extended family in India. As a result, I was convinced that I would enjoy a comparable level of success by following their example.

Unfortunately, due to the demands of the store, my parents viewed my work there as a higher priority than my education. Consequently, I often skipped classes and worked late into the night when my father was short-handed. Everything changed in 2009, when he collapsed at the store and died from a heart attack. In subsequent days, we learned that the trappings of success that we had enjoyed were all an illusion; beyond the assets in the store, there was no money or life insurance to pay our ongoing expenses. Instead, we were forced to close the store and sell the inventory for pennies on the dollar. A year later, we moved into a homeless shelter when the bank foreclosed on the home that my parents had worked so hard to buy.

This life-changing event taught me a powerful lesson in humility. In an instant, we went from successful entrepreneurs to grieving survivors who relied upon public assistance. Although I was grateful for the help that we received, I was determined to acquire the education I would need to support my family and serve as an example for others. Balancing a job with the demands of my classes presented formidable time and logistical challenges. Nevertheless, I was determined to set a positive example for my siblings by handling them with grace and dignity.

I also discovered that my family's problems were far from unique. In our minority neighborhood, formal education is rarely a priority. As a result, few children have the academic training and practical experience they need to make wise decisions about their future. Like many children from immigrant families, I struggled to succeed in an educational system with which my parents were not familiar. Fortunately, I had a strong support system in Cicero's Indian-American community, which kept me focused on my long-term goals.

Next month, I will proudly graduate from Syracuse University with a perfect GPA. I have also received scholarship awards from the YWCA, the Elk Society, and the Middle Eastern Academic Symposium. I would never have received these honors without the support of my family, friends, teachers, and mentors, who had tremendous faith in my ability to create a better future. They also ignited my desire to share the benefits of my education with those who have not enjoyed similar opportunities.

Far too often, the kids in my neighborhood are forced to drop out of school in order to support their families. Without the benefits of a college degree, they cannot obtain a good job or build a successful life. As someone who was fortunate enough to escape a dead-end existence, I am determined to pave a clear path for others to do the same.

Today, because of my support system, I have escaped the temptations of drugs and violence that plague the streets of Cicero. Most importantly, I have realized that education is the only path to a safe and successful future, in which there truly are no limits. After medical school, I hope to launch a non-profit organization that serves the needs of inner city children. By doing so, I can find practical ways to transform communities through the power of a positive example. At the very least, I can encourage other children to stay in school and fulfill their academic potential.

Our Assessment: This candidate faced formidable obstacles to graduate from college, support his family, and build a successful life. By positioning himself as a survivor (rather than a victim), he gained considerable respect from the committee, who knew that he had the strength and tenacity to help others succeed.

Your Contribution to the Program's Diversity

Last fall, I participated in a humanitarian mission trip that literally transformed my life. I accompanied five members of the International Red Cross team to Darfur, where we assisted civilians who were displaced by the war between the government and the indigenous population. Upon my arrival, I witnessed the ongoing threats that the residents endure, including poverty, disease, malnutrition, and random violence. On my first day, a military official showed us how to identify, extract, and de-activate a landmine. He also explained how to protect ourselves if we encountered an armed terrorist. These experiences showed me the daily reality of the locals, who were trapped in a violent world in which the danger was impossible to predict.

The following day, we distributed dry rations, new clothes, and school supplies at an orphanage that housed more than 100 survivors of the recent violence. A number of the children had lost not only their homes, but their entire family. It was humbling to know that the supplies we delivered, including vitamins, antibiotics, and bandages, could be used to save a life.

Throughout our trip, we spent considerable time traveling among the various facilities that needed our help. After our trip to the orphanage, we visited a makeshift Red Cross Hospital in Darfur, which had been previously destroyed by a terrorist attack. Along the way, we stopped at camps that provided temporary shelter for people who were displaced by the civil war. According to our team leader, who had visited the same camps a year before, hundreds of occupants had already found permanent rehabilitation. However, we also spoke to several people who were still waiting for a safe place to live, and were forced to stay in overcrowded camps that lack clean water, healthy food, sanitary conditions, and security. Not surprisingly, in this unhealthy and impoverished environment, few people have hope for a safe future.

In our free time, we helped our host family with their small farming business, which bore little resemblance to the industrial facilities in developed nations. With no money, machinery, or fertilizer, the farmers in Darfur rely upon rain, hard work, and the power of their cattle to plough the soil. Their yield, of course, is dependent upon the amount of rainfall the area receives; during times of drought, the farmers barely make enough money to survive. As I watched them work, I was amazed by their ability to move quickly and easily through the thick mud. The volunteers, in contrast, struggled to take a single step in these intense conditions. When I removed my boots at the end of the day, I had a newfound appreciation for the labor required to harvest a single serving of food.

On my long ride home, I realized how blessed I am to live in a safe home with a loving family that has the physical, financial, and emotional support to face life's challenges. In contrast, the people in Darfur, through no fault of their own, struggle arduously simply to survive. By volunteering for the International Red Cross, I fulfilled my desire to visit a part of my continent that had been completely alien to me. As summer begins, I am eager to visit the region again, to continue the work for such a noble cause. Surely, in medical school, I can convince my fellow students to support similar humanitarian initiatives, which serve the needs of deserving residents of the war-torn regions of Africa.

Our Assessment: This essay revealed the candidate's observations of a war-torn area, where the residents struggle to survive. His commitment to helping them, which is confirmed in the final paragraph of his essay, confirms that this trip made a lasting impact on his life.

Your Contribution to the Program's Diversity

According to the medical school selection criteria, I am completely "average." I am a young man from an upper middle class Chicago family. I attended a private Catholic high school, where I was top of the class; my GPA and MCAT scores are acceptable, but not particularly noteworthy.

Some say that I blossomed during my four years at Loyola College, while others say that I "found myself." I prefer to think that I seized the chance to fulfill my own potential. When I couldn't decide whether to major in biology or chemistry, I opted to complete a dual degree in both disciplines. Even though it meant a sizable increase in my workload, I was undeterred. I loved both subjects and felt that I had a lot to learn. Four years later, armed with two degrees and ton of motivation, I feel I have a lot to contribute. My career aspirations are anything but average.

Throughout my four years of college, I juggled my demanding course load with several rewarding activities that confirmed my fit for medicine. At the coroner's office, I helped to autopsy bodies from death scenes, where I also gathered evidence. As a volunteer, I held the hand of a surgical patient just before she was wheeled into the operating room. I also published two articles on fatty acid metabolism and placed 23rd in the Boston Marathon.

But then again, all candidates have accomplishments that are important to them. Perhaps that is why I am able to feel extraordinary and average at the same time, because I am from a family in which accomplishment is the norm. In my house, attending college was never a question. Pursuing a career in medicine is not only supported, but expected. In my world, in which both parents are cardiac physicians, it is unthinkable to settle for anything less than my absolute best. And I am fine with that.

Technically, I could claim minority status, because my parents were both born and raised in Costa Rica. Technically, I could call myself Latino, but I don't, because that is not how I choose to define myself. In my mind, my "diversity" is not defined by my parents' experiences sixty years ago. Instead, it is defined by the breadth and quality of my experiences as a chemist, biologist, volunteer, caregiver, author and hiker. I can do many things well, with passion, all at the same time. Most importantly, I am not only open to new ideas and experiences, but eager to seek them out. This is what differentiates me.

<u>Our Assessment</u>: Many times, non-minority candidates ask us how they can possibly write a compelling diversity statement. This example shows them how. To us, the most impressive aspect of this statement is the final paragraph, which reveals the candidate's reluctance to focus on his race. Instead, he wrote a strong statement about his myriad accomplishments, which were an excellent fit for medical school.

Your Contribution to the Program's Diversity

As I entered the Salvation Army building in the heart of Baghdad, I pondered the meaning of its motto, Blood and Fire. Was it, I wondered, the mantra of a secret cult or the symbol of war and violence? And why did they need a teacher who spoke both English and Arabic – would my students be spies or soldiers? Before I could contemplate this mystery, a man approached me and extended his right hand. "Hello, young lady. I am Major Clark. The students are eager to begin."

As we entered the classroom, I saw a dozen people of various ages sitting in a circle. They smiled tentatively, which suggested that they shared my apprehension about this new educational experience. Before he left, Major Clark whispered some words of encouragement. "Your students, they definitely need your help. Right now, they don't know a word of English." As he disappeared in the hallway, I sought comfort from my father's advice, "It's OK to be scared. Just work through it."

When I accepted my position as a volunteer teacher at the Salvation Army, I felt unprepared for the social or educational challenges that it would present. At 18, I was the child of an American diplomat who had been raised in the Middle East and educated at an international school in Baghdad. As I awaited my visas to attend college in the United States, I searched for a position that would allow me to use my linguistic skills in a fun and creative way. The job at the Salvation Army seemed to fit the bill. Yet, upon meeting Major Clark, I had a troubling revelation: everyone I knew spoke at least a little English. Was I truly prepared to teach a roomful of students who didn't?

Thankfully, on my first day, I followed my heart and taught them the first word that came to mind: Hello. Afterwards, with the help of my extremely motivated students, everything fell into place. Our year of classes passed swiftly and productively. "John, this is great! 98 out of 100! Be careful with your spelling, though. The number is spelled t-w-o, not t-o." John widened his eyes and scratched his head when he realized his mistake. Behind him, Laura, who was a spunky 50-year-old with red hair and blue eyeliner, looked guilty and elusive as I passed her desk to review her assignment. Obviously, her dog had eaten her homework.

Over time, as the students mastered the nuances of English, their success ignited my passion for teaching. Rose, who initially could not state her name, could now describe her family and school. Ken earned the highest marks for English in his entire school, which was a tremendous honor. And Kim, who was originally too scared to speak, recited a poem in English at her father's funeral. A year after I first entered the Salvation Army building, I finally realized that the "Fire" on the logo was my burning desire to help my students succeed. Now, I needed to discover the meaning of the word "Blood."

A month ago, I pondered my father's words about fear as I waited for my students to arrive. This time, however, I was not afraid to teach them, but to announce that I was leaving. As I broke the news about my plans to attend college in the US, Major Clark entered the room. He reassured the students that they could continue to improve their linguistic skills at the Salvation Army after I departed; he would find them a new English teacher who was "just like me."

The Major's words, however well-intentioned, pierced my heart like a sharp needle. In an instant, I understood that the bond between my students and me – and my hard-won satisfaction as a teacher - was the elusive "Blood" in the Salvation Army motto. And breaking that bond was more painful than I could ever imagine. In our final weeks together, I cherished every moment with my eclectic group of students, who have placed their trust in me as a teacher, friend, and role model. Their long educational journey, including the laughs, tears, and frustrations of learning a new language, is a tangible reminder of the "Blood and Fire" that fuels all of our accomplishments.

<u>Our Assessment</u>: This candidate took a risk by writing about a volunteer experience that had nothing to do with medicine. By doing so, she presented an experience that the committee would never have known about any other way. From our perspective, that is what a diversity statement is for – to show the reader a balanced perspective of the many skills and experiences that you will bring to their program.

Most Meaningful Clinical Experience

In 2003, I lost my mother to a virulent form of ovarian cancer, which claimed her life within three months of her initial diagnosis. Since then, I have felt a strong affinity with patients who struggle with the same disease. With this in mind, I volunteered in the oncology ward at the University of Barcelona Medical Center, which is known for its aggressive experimental treatment regimens for ovarian cancer. During my time there, I worked closely with several patients and served as a translator for doctors from the United States. By interacting with the researchers, I learned about several promising experimental techniques that are being evaluated in Europe, including isotopes and gene therapy. On a personal level, I also formed meaningful friendships with the patients who obtained chemotherapy at our facility. Using my fluency in both English and Spanish, I shared my experience of being an aspiring oncologist and the daughter of a cancer survivor. Many times, I simply listened in silence as the patients shared their hopes and fears for the future. Although my patients in Barcelona were from a dramatically different culture, we shared a powerful bond in our fight against a common disease. By making these personal connections, I discovered the power of friendship and compassion in a patient's recovery.

<u>Our Assessment</u>: This candidate's greatest challenge was consolidating her story to meet an unusually short length restriction, which required her to eliminate most of the details and focus on her overall experience. The resulting draft is short, honest, and heartfelt.

Most Meaningful Clinical Experience

My greatest talent is fundraising on behalf of cancer research. My inspiration comes directly from the heart. As a child, I watched helplessly as my mother waged a long battle against breast cancer, which required her to endure a grueling cycle of surgery, chemotherapy and radiation. I quickly learned that her "pathology" results revealed the success or failure of her treatment regimens. Like my parents, I feared "bad" results (metastasis) and rejoiced when she received "good" reports (tumor shrinkage). Despite my initial trepidation, I was determined to understand as much as possible about the disease. Ultimately, my mother's illness inspired me to pursue a career as a public health advocate.

As an adult, I have raised funds for several charities that promote cancer awareness in my community. Between 2008 and 2010, I raised over $4 million for the Dallas chapter of Gilda's Club, which offers free services and educational programs for cancer patients, survivors and their families. I am currently organizing a gala benefit on behalf of Los Angeles Oncology Associates, which offers free and reduced price services to indigent and uninsured patients. I also volunteer at the center, where I draw blood, conduct lab analyses, take vitals, assist with bone marrow procedures and provide emotional support to chemotherapy patients. Thanks to my early experiences as a caregiver, I understand the challenges that patients endure on their uneasy road to recovery. I can't imagine a better use of my time or energy.

<u>Our Assessment</u>: Rather than focus on her clinical work, this candidate opted to include her accomplishments as a fundraiser for breast cancer research. By explaining her motivation for this work, along with the depth and breadth of her commitment, she proved her sincerity to the reader – and her effectiveness as a health care advocate.

Most Meaningful Research Experience

There I slouched, in a crowded waiting room that was filled with sick and elderly patients. Normally, on this bright summer day, I would still be sound asleep in my bed, but not today. Instead, I rose early and drove to my appointment at UCLA Medical Center. After several minutes, I heard a voice exclaim, "Peter, come on in!" I stepped forward and shook the hand of my future research professor, Dr. Brian Smith, who was the head of neurological research. Although I didn't know it at the time, our work with autistic patients that summer would become the most influential experience of my life.

Working at a top tier medical facility opened my eyes to personal and professional opportunities that I never knew existed. The first week, I reviewed several reputable journal articles about the onset of autism. Then, I observed the ongoing testing in Dr. Smith's lab, to determine the impact of early intervention with toddlers who had autistic spectrum disorder. Every day, after I recorded the results of each test, I would compile the data into a statistical database; every week, I would present my findings at our departmental meetings, in which a group of researchers conferred with several staff neurologists. After I recited the patient's symptoms and the impact of various behavioral and nutritional therapies, the panel would evaluate the information and make recommendations for future treatments. The goal, as always, was to find some way to reach the mind of these deserving patients, who were locked in a world that seemed impossible to penetrate.

As an aspiring neurologist, I was invigorated by the chance to work with patients and gain first-hand insight into the structure of cognition. My weekly meetings with the physicians revealed a detailed perspective of human thought and behavior that I could not have acquired any other way. They also sparked a personal and professional epiphany. When I accepted the position, I was a shy teenager who questioned my ability to make a difference in the world. By the end of the summer, I knew that I was destined for a medical career.

As part of my job, I also completed my own projects under the direction of Dr. Smith. The purity of the research – and the passion of my peers – was downright inspirational. Everyone I met was there for the same reason – to conduct state-of-the-art research in a discipline they loved. Whenever possible, I seized the chance to discuss medical advances and theories with noted experts in the field. Only later did I realize how much these interactions had changed me.

After all of the testing, statistical analyses, and departmental meetings, I held a powerful ideal that I had not previously harbored – that I could use my skills to make a meaningful difference in society. To the people in the lab, I was not a naive "college kid," but a devoted researcher with something to contribute. Their faith and support gave me the confidence to see myself through more noble and ambitious eyes. Eventually, as a neurologist, I hope to continue their fine work and provide my patients with the compassionate care they deserve. After working closely with the researchers, physicians, and support staff at UCLA Medical Center, I could not ask for more positive or inspirational role models.

Our Assessment: In this secondary essay, the candidate discussed his summer research in a lab that investigated the causes of autism. The information complemented the material in his primary statement, which presented his volunteer work at a local hospital. To reinforce his accomplishments, the candidate asked Dr. Smith to write a letter of recommendation on his behalf, which provided a detailed account of his organizational and interpersonal skills.

Most Challenging Volunteer Experience

"I would rather do *anything* than sit here and read." When I joined Helping Hands, which is a mentorship at Pomona College, I was prepared for the challenges of working with disadvantaged children who had fallen behind in the classroom. But nothing had prepared me for the belligerence I encountered from Sheryl, the 12-year-old girl who had been assigned to me.

After her bold announcement, I struggled to get our relationship on track. Unfortunately, my initial tactic, which was to cite the benefits and enjoyment of reading, fell on deaf ears. To Sheryl, my childhood memories of Judy Blume's novels could not compete with the social allure of middle school. "I could be at the beach with my friends right now. Why should I stay here with you?"

When I looked in Sheryl's eyes, I realized that she was testing me; I also realized that I only had one chance to win her confidence and get her interested in reading. So, I did what any self-respecting mentor would do – I bribed her with candy. From the moment I walked in the room, Sheryl had eyed the Hershey Kisses in my purse. In a moment of desperation, I made a deal with her. If Sheryl would work with me for an hour, I would split my candy with her. We shook hands and got to work.

During our first session, I realized that Sheryl's bravado masked a keen intelligence and a genuine desire to learn. Unfortunately, she had fallen behind in her classes and was reluctant to look "stupid" by asking her teacher for help. I assured Sheryl that she was anything but stupid and that I would do whatever was necessary to help her read at grade level.

In developing a lesson plan, I kept our goals challenging yet realistic. First, we read stories that were beneath her grade level, to build her confidence and expand her vocabulary. Gradually, Sheryl was confident enough to tackle harder books with more complex themes and characters. As the months wore on, I taught Sheryl how to answer tough exam questions about a story's theme or message, which required a higher level of insight. Her sensitivity to the material genuinely surprised me. By the end of the year, Sheryl had read the first three *Harry Potter* series, which included a particularly sophisticated vocabulary. Most importantly, she had raised her Reading grade from an F to a B and applied for a library card.

For our last session, I brought Sheryl a heartfelt gift; a bag of Hersey Kisses and a copy of *Harry Potter and the Half-Blood Prince*. I was humbled when she handed me her own gift in return: a hand-drawn card that said, "Thank you for helping me to read. It's more fun than I expected."

The following year, when I recruited new students to join Helping Hands, I tried to give them an honest assessment of what they could gain from becoming a mentor. Like Sheryl, many of the children in the program have personal, financial, and educational problems that make them difficult to teach. Some of the barriers, such as linguistic deficiencies and a lack of support at home, can be nearly impossible to overcome. But the rewards of reaching a student like Sheryl – one day lesson at a time – were more fulfilling than I ever imagined.

Ironically, I probably gained more from our relationship than Sheryl did. Thanks to her, I learned how to connect with someone whose life was very different from mine. I also learned how to adjust my teaching strategy to suit her needs and expectations, rather than my own. By the end of our year together, I recognized that I had not only taught Sheryl how to read, but I had opened her mind to an entire world of possibilities that she might never have considered. The Hershey Kisses were just an added bonus.

Our Assessment: In her primary statement, this candidate discussed her volunteer work in a clinical setting; as a result, she decided to show a different side of herself in this essay. The casual style, combined with her judicious use of quotes, made it particularly memorable.

Most Meaningful Research Experience

"Be as quiet as possible. Too much noise tends to distract him." As I followed my advisor into the clinic, I wondered what I had gotten myself into. Suddenly, being a summer researcher didn't seem like such a "cushy job." On my first day at Brown University's Unit for Experimental Psychiatry, I found myself in the psych ward at Rhode Island Hospital, where our first patient was a 40-year-old named Brad. At first glance, he seemed like nice enough guy, but his chart told a different story: repeated hospitalizations for paranoid schizophrenia, which had resisted conventional treatments. According to my advisor, Brad had attacked the previous researcher because he disliked the incessant ring of the woman's cell phone. I made a mental note to put mine on vibrate before I entered the building.

Although I expected to do my independent research in the computer lab, I accepted the assignment in the psychiatric ward to test my affinity for patient care. It was my first actual exposure to mental illness; on my first day, I wondered if I was up to the challenge. Fortunately, as a novice, I started on the easier assignments related to nutritional therapy. For 28 consecutive days, I monitored a lab in which patients with schizophrenia and clinical depression were given a mega-dose of XXXXX to test its effect on their mood. Later, the patients were also given varying types and doses of psychotropic drugs to determine if there was a cumulative effect of XXXXX over time. In addition to its obvious benefits to the drug companies, the data would also benefit the patients with schizophrenia whose conditions had defied conventional treatment. Somewhere in our protocol, we might discover a way that XXXXX could help them.

Working in the hospital required me to perfect my communication skills, while sorting, collating, and analyzing my data improved my organizational skills. To achieve my objective, I had to write an original computer program to handle more than one million individual data points. Facing the daunting prospect of entering more than one thousand lines of computer code required me to find new approaches to an intricate problem. After evaluating various alternatives, I eventually decided to tackle the project by breaking it into a number of smaller goals that I could manage individually. Even using the most efficient approach, the data entry required six weeks of concentrated effort for me to complete.

My work in the Experimental Psychiatry ward taught me valuable problem solving skills. In hindsight, I believe that both my engineering education and my experience applying it to psychological research will be valuable in the study and practice of medicine. The questions and problems I will encounter in medical research will have numerous possible answers, which will require me to evaluate and choose among several possible directions. In my study at the hospital, I had many options for each variable under investigation: Which patients should receive which drugs? In what dosage? Should we have a control group? A placebo? What computer program should I use for my data analysis? How should I structure the program? To organize and conduct the study properly, I had to carefully construct a logical argument for each choice, using relevant information about each parameter. My analytical ability, which I developed through courses in psychology, statistics and engineering, and improved through practical applications, allowed me to develop and defend solid answers to these questions. Hopefully, the same skill will continue to be helpful throughout my medical career.

As I prepare for medical school, the definitive results of my study at Brown have yet to be published. To properly evaluate the efficacy of XXXXX, the team must conduct thousands of trials using patients of all ages, which will likely take several more years. Looking back, I am proud to have been a part of such an important and challenging piece of work, which taught me how to define and solve a complex research problem. More importantly, it gave me the confidence to work with mentally ill patients who are in dire need of more effective treatments. I look forward to challenging and perfecting these skills at Harvard Medical School.

Our Assessment: This candidate was an engineering major who had no intention of pursuing a medical career. In this statement, he explains how his summer research project at Brown changed his perspective about his career goals. Combined with his primary statement, which discussed his clinical experience, he gave the committee a balanced perspective of his background and skills.

Describe your Life / Medical Practice in 10 Years

My personal definition of success includes a happy family, a challenging career, and an opportunity to make a lasting contribution in my community. Throughout the next ten years, I plan to fully develop my potential in each of these areas.

I can only reach my full potential with the love and support of my family and friends, who contribute greatly to my academic accomplishments and personal happiness. My parents have provided unconditional support for my endeavors; they have also encouraged me to adhere to the highest moral and ethical standards. At every stage of my development, I could not have asked for better role models. I am also blessed with several good friends who encourage me to fulfill my dreams. In the next ten years, I plan to sustain these connections, marry my fiancé, and raise a family of my own.

On a professional level, I am committed to the lifelong education that the medical profession requires. Through my research in electrophysiology and clinical neuroscience, I had the opportunity to use emerging technologies to solve scientific problems. I plan to continue this pursuit in medical school, to stay abreast of the exciting new developments in neuroscience. Ten years from now, I hope to be a neurosurgeon at a large teaching hospital, where I can help to train aspiring physicians. To do so, I must cultivate the leadership and administrative skills I will need to lead a surgical department at a world class facility.

I am also committed to serving my community as a public health advocate. By volunteering at my local hospital, I have observed the practical and spiritual aspects of a medical career. I plan to be an effective physician who demonstrates compassion, dedication and diligence to those who entrust their care to me. I also plan to continue my work as a youth advocate, which is particularly rewarding. As a Native American, I struggled with feelings of uncertainty and prejudice throughout my academic career. Looking ahead, I hope to become a role model for other young minorities who are pursuing their own professional dreams. By teaching, lecturing, writing and volunteer work, I plan to share my expertise with others in my community.

Medicine is a challenging career that requires much from those who choose it. I am confident that my determination and passion for the field will enable me to fulfill my aspirations.

Our Assessment: This essay worked because the author made a direct link between his own experiences to his goals in research and public health. He also cited his personal aspirations, which revealed his need for balance and his commitment to his family.

Describe your Life / Medical Practice in 10 Years

In ten years, I plan to be a practicing surgeon who balances my professional responsibilities with hobbies, a strong family life, and volunteer work in my community. My interest in a surgical career dates back to age eleven, when my younger brother severed his finger in a boating accident. Just a few hours later, I saw a surgeon repair the damage at the local hospital. Working under a microscope, he used minute sutures to reattach my brother's finger, while he explained each step to my worried parents. I was mesmerized by the surgeon's knowledge, skill, and caring demeanor. A week later, when the bandage came off, I was further impressed by the end result: my brother's finger shows no evidence of serious injury. To an 11-year-old girl, the surgeon's work was nothing short of magic.

I explored my interest in surgery as a medical volunteer and researcher. During my sophomore year, I spent the fall term shadowing a cardiothoracic surgeon at the University of Kansas Medical Center. Besides observing surgeries, I also attended rounds and assisted with experimental procedures in the animal laboratory. Dr. Smith, who ran the lab, took the time to explain the nuances of different surgical methods. By operating on animals, I discovered that surgery requires a unique combination of academic knowledge, physical skill, and patience; it also requires creativity, imagination and the ability to develop practical solutions on a moment's notice. Accordingly, I plan to spend the next several years developing these skills.

Like the surgeon I met in the emergency room at age 11, I intend to serve my patients with humility and respect. That surgeon's dedication, coupled with his ability to comfort us, inspires me to be physician who is both capable and compassionate. Although I haven't selected a specialty area, I am intrigued by the current developments in neurosurgery, which are a great fit for my academic background in biochemistry and neuroscience. As part of my medical school curriculum, I hope to explore relevant opportunities in these areas.

I am also committed to making a contribution to medical research and education. Based on my experiences at Harvard University and the University of Kansas, I am receptive to working in a teaching environment, where I will conduct and publish independent research. A dedicated volunteer, I am also eager to offer my professional skills to patients who are unable to obtain traditional medical care. As a practicing physician, I will assume an active role in my community as a leader in public health and a proponent of preventive medicine.

In my quest to be a good doctor, I must also remain a balanced person. To this end, I will continue to pursue my passion for running, painting, and social occasions with my family. A balanced life will enhance my productivity at work and be crucial to my professional success. Thus, in ten years, I plan to be both a practicing physician and a practicing human who is equally committed to personal and professional excellence.

Our Assessment: By telling the story about her brother's injury, this candidate had a creative opening for her essay that was relevant and memorable. Then, she backed up her goals with relevant academic, research, and clinical experiences. The essay was well perceived.

Describe your Life / Medical Practice in 10 Years

My ultimate goal is to be a practicing neurologist who specializes in the treatment of Bell's Palsy. My initial interest in medicine was ignited by my own battle with this mysterious illness during my senior year in high school. Over a period of three days, I lost control of the right side of my face and the movement of my right arm. These sudden physical changes were traumatic, yet the emotional consequences were equally compelling. Before my illness, I was an excellent student and the captain of the football team. After my symptoms emerged, my friends had difficulty looking at me the same way. When my condition failed to improve over time, I wondered if I would ever be my "old self" again.

Unfortunately, my family doctor had limited information on Bell's Palsy and no guaranteed treatment regimen. Unwilling to wait for the symptoms to subside, I investigated the disease on my own. As I perused the medical literature, I discovered that the experts didn't seem to fully understand Bell's Palsy. There was no known cure, yet I found information about a new drug that reportedly would hasten my recovery. I presented with my findings to my neurologist, who approved the drug. With the aid of this medication, I recovered fully within several weeks.

As a pre-med major, I enjoyed numerous opportunities to conduct independent research, both on campus and in clinical settings. Every project centered on the possible causes, treatments and cures for Bell's Palsy. Neurologists are still uncertain about its specific cause, because the disease is seemingly random in occurrence and duration. From my own experience, the symptoms recur at will and respond erratically to drug therapy. During my summer internship at Beth Israel Hospital, I participated in two clinical trials that examined the effects of diet and exercise on the disease. Our results suggest that long-term mega-doses of Vitamin A may prevent the onset of the symptoms of Bell's Palsy in patients of average height and weight. We also discovered that there may be a genetic component to the disease.

In my eventual practice, I plan to specialize in the treatment of neurological abnormalities such as Bell's Palsy, which are under-investigated because they only strike a few thousand patients per year. As one of them, I am dedicated to finding a cure. Ironically, my illness helped me to realize my suitability for medicine; it also forced me to rely on an internal compass that I didn't know existed. By managing my illness, I became less focused on external appearances and more appreciative of people's feelings and inner beauty. I also developed a tolerance for strangers, whose quizzical looks were not evil or judgmental, but simply an indication of their own lack of understanding. Through my internship at Beth Israel Hospital, I also established a terrific rapport with the other patients in the clinical trials whose "war stories" were similar to my own.

Over time, Bell's Palsy gave me a unique appreciation for the emotional aspects of illness, which will allow me to be more sympathetic to the feelings of others. Ultimately, by surviving this disease, I gained a sense of purpose and direction that I could never have acquired any other way. I am excited by the opportunity to share the lessons I have learned with my patients and colleagues throughout my medical career.

Our Assessment: By discussing his battle with Bell's Palsy, this candidate gave the reader keen insight into his motivation and character, which was confirmed by his recommendation letters. His goals were perfectly aligned with his own experiences.

Describe your Life / Medical Practice in 10 Years

After landing in Beijing, I visited a Buddhist temple in my father's native village. Along the way, I saw dozens of people washing their bodies in the adjacent river. At first, I was humbled by their need to bathe in public; upon closer examination, I became overwhelmed by sadness. The murky water, which was their only source of "cleanliness," was teeming with insects and parasites. In an instant, I understood the source of the mysterious illnesses that plagued the local residents. With little money for medical care – and an unsanitary water supply – even simple infections became impossible to cure.

For the first time, I truly understood why my parents had moved from China and San Francisco. The poverty and disease in their native country filled me with guilt and frustration. As a citizen from a privileged nation, I enjoyed medical and financial blessings that my extended family would never see. Why, then, were people in developing nations allowed to remain sick and hungry? Each day, as I wandered the village streets, I was consumed with a single desire: to find a way to alleviate people's suffering.

When I returned to the U.S., my passion for science and my yearning to help others assumed a new sense of urgency. Before my trip, I was not sure how I could use my skills to best serve society. Afterwards, I realized that I could have a significant impact on a disadvantaged population by becoming a physician. In 2008, I spent the summer as a volunteer for Compassionate Intervention, which is an NGO in rural China that works with indigent patients with HIV/AIDS. There, I met a woman named LingLi, who contracted HIV from her unfaithful husband. By the time she was diagnosed, LingLi had unknowingly transmitted the virus to her daughter Mioki through her infected breast milk. I was humbled – and outraged – to learn that LingLi had no other way to feed her child. In this impoverished community, the cost of baby formula was well beyond her reach, yet LingLi handled her burden with an uncommon grace; she repeatedly expressed her gratitude for the care that we provided.

LingLi's situation plagued me with difficult philosophical questions. Why did AIDS continue to proliferate in poor and developing nations? What future would LingLi and Mioki face without the services of Compassionate Intervention? As I earned their trust – and returned their heartfelt hugs - I realized that I had the power to make a difference. By pursuing a career in international medicine, I can provide a source of physical, educational, and emotional support to people like LingLi and Mioki, who deserve the best possible care.

After working with underprivileged patients in China – and sharing their medical, social, and political stigma, I was inspired to become an advocate on their behalf. When I returned to school, I organized a seminar that explained how students could help AIDS patients across the globe. I also attended a national conference for members of Compassionate Intervention, which taught me practical ways to fight against global health injustices. The group's goal of providing quality medical care in underserved areas resonated strongly within me on a personal basis.

After medical school, I hope to obtain a Masters in Public Health and support the clinical and research initiatives of the World Health Organization. By doing so, I can provide a voice for people who do not have access to medical care, including 20% of the U.S. population. Margaret Mead once noted that "a small group of thoughtful, committed citizens can change the world." As a physician, I will promote a spirit of solidarity in medicine, and work to make health care more accessible to the people who need it the most. As citizens of the earth, they deserve nothing less.

Our Assessment: This candidate had a longer length limit for this question, which allowed him to tell the story about his visit to China and his work for Compassionate Intervention, which inspired his desire to pursue a career in public health. The personal nature of these stories, combined with the eloquent yet accessible writing style, made a positive impression on the committee.

Chapter 7: Essays That Target a Specific School

Nearly every medical school has a secondary essay question that asks students why they have selected that particular school. On a practical basis, the decision is usually based on cost, location, and statistics; most students apply to the schools where they think they have a realistic chance of getting in. Unfortunately, it is rarely in your best interest to state that in your answer. Instead, you should show the committee that you have done your homework by drafting an essay that matches your specific strengths to what their program has to offer. Good points to include:

- The strength of their coursework
- Their educational approach or philosophy
- Your desire to conduct research with a particular professor (or in a specific area)
- The strength of their clinical affiliations

What you write will also depend on the length limit that the school has imposed. Some allow a full page, while others only allow a few lines. Whatever word, page, or character limit you face, you must match your goals with each school's strengths and objectives.

Here are several secondary essays that answer the question "why our school." To protect the privacy of the applicant, the names of all people, classes, schools, places, and companies have been changed.

Why Our School

For a variety of reasons, Harvard Medical School is my first choice for my medical education. First, the program takes a holistic approach to health care, which treats the whole person, rather than a symptom or disease. After working in a clinical setting, I am convinced that this is the best way to achieve a positive outcome. By studying the personal, cultural, and socioeconomic factors that influence health, I will be able to see the "big picture" when I make a diagnosis.

Second, I am eager to complete my education in the heart of Boston, where I will have the opportunity to form positive relationships with patients of different ages, backgrounds, and experiences. By serving the needs of this heterogeneous population, I will be exposed to a variety of people and conditions that I would not encounter in a rural setting. Additionally, the program offers a chance for me to continue my training in Spanish, which I have pursued for the past few years. By improving my familiarity with the Spanish language and culture, I will be better prepared to serve this rapidly growing demographic group.

Third, Harvard offers exemplary training in both the clinical and research aspects of medicine. By working with patients during my first year of studies, I can put my classroom knowledge to immediate use. I am eager to learn the best ways to serve their needs in an efficient and compassionate manner. Additionally, the program offers an opportunity for me to develop and research new treatments. By staying abreast of the latest advancements – and participating in their evaluation, I can ensure that my patients receive the most promising treatment options.

Fourth, through its affiliation with the College of Public Health, Harvard shares my passion for serving disadvantaged communities. In 2010, I worked as a health care volunteer in an impoverished village in rural India. By doing so, I gained a realistic perspective of the barriers to health care in underserved areas. Unfortunately, due to my limited clinical experience, I did not have the knowledge to help the patients with their ailments. Harvard Medical School offers a chance for me to fill this void in a positive way. As part of my medical education, I plan to contribute to local, national, and global initiatives that promote the benefits of preventive medicine and health education. Ideally, I will also learn how to promote relevant policies that improve the quality of health care on a national level. By understanding the barriers to health care delivery, I will be better prepared to serve the patients in my own community.

Finally, through its extraordinary clinical affiliations in Massachusetts, Harvard emphasizes the importance of compassionate patient care, which is the true spirit of medicine; it also attracts candidates who view medicine as a lifelong calling, rather than simply a job. I am eager to attend a school that exemplifies these values and priorities. By completing my education at Harvard Medical School, I will have the chance to work with – and learn from – distinguished experts in numerous medical specialties. Afterwards, I will be well prepared to complete a challenging residency program, launch my own practice, and serve my community in a compassionate and responsible manner.

<u>Our Assessment</u>: This candidate explained his interest in Harvard in a logical and well-organized way. He also personalized the essay by citing his fluency in Spanish and his volunteer work in India. The resulting essay was well perceived.

Why Our School

When I evaluated prospective medical schools, I limited my search to universities with exceptional programs in dermatology, which is my intended area of specialization. I also sought programs with a demonstrated commitment to research, including opportunities to participate at the graduate level. Finally, I wanted a program that offered exemplary clinical training in a variety of hospitals and settings, to prepare for the challenges of my eventual practice. With its outstanding faculty, state-of-the-art facilities, and world-class research team, the University of Florida Medical School quickly emerged as my first choice.

UFMS offers several unique benefits, including the opportunity to train at the prestigious Florida Dermatological Research Institute with physicians and faculty members who are national and international leaders in their fields. Through relevant classes, research, and clinical rotations, I will acquire exceptional training in advanced diagnostic and treatment techniques, including the safe and ethical use of cosmetic facial fillers to counter the effects of aging. Additionally, I will have ample opportunity to explore different specialties within dermatology in the many fine hospitals and institutes that are affiliated with the program.

As a resident of Florida for seventeen years, I am also attracted to the school's location, which is in close proximity to my extended family. Their presence will enhance my transition to the area, on both a personal and financial basis. Finally, my familiarity with the political, social, and economic environment in Florida will enable me to help other students adjust to the area; by doing so, I will form personal and professional relationships that will literally last a lifetime.

<u>Our Assessment</u>: This is a great answer that adhered to the school's rigid length limit – it provided a lot of information in a logical and concise manner.

Why Our School

As a student and researcher, I tend to create my own path. Rather than accept the status quo, I eagerly embrace new ways to serve the needs of my patients. In the medical community, the University of Central Florida Medical School (UCFMS) represents an exciting leap into the future. This brand new program, which offers a progressive curriculum and state-of-the-art learning facility, will allow me to be a "pioneer" in preventive health education.

Compared to other programs, UCFMS offers several distinct benefits. By integrating clinical experiences with traditional classroom lectures early in the program, UCFMS enables its students to reinforce what they learn by applying their knowledge in practical situations. This healthy balance between theory and practice is essential to my success as a physician. As a prospective student, I am particularly attracted to the Build-A-Bridge Mentorship Program, which will enable me to shadow a primary care physician during my first two years of medical school. This exposure will greatly enhance my learning experience and provide an invaluable source of information and feedback.

I am also eager to participate in the Bridge-To-You Program, which brings the resources of the medical school to underserved locations. By providing patients with easy access to affordable care, I can promote the benefits of early intervention and improve their chances for a positive outcome. UCFMS will also teach me how to develop and implement public health programs in disadvantaged communities, which highlight the benefits of preventive care and health education. By launching these programs and promoting awareness about them, I can become a trusted and reliable presence in the communities where I am needed the most.

After studying, researching, and working in diverse academic settings, I know that every medical school has a distinct mission and culture. Last fall, I have the privilege of interviewing at UCFMS and speaking to several students and faculty members. The camaraderie on campus, which values collaboration over competition, is an excellent match for my personal learning style. I am excited by the possibility of learning from – and among – those who share my commitment to inner city medicine. After exploring the nuances of different medical schools, I feel most comfortable with the goals, culture, and expectations at UCFMS. If given a chance, I will make a unique contribution to your program.

<u>Our Assessment</u>: This essay is strong, focused, and detailed. By matching her interests to the strengths of the program, the candidate showed the committee that she was a perfect fit for what they had to offer.

Why Our School

The curriculum at UC-Davis offers a holistic approach to medicine, which treats the whole person, rather than a symptom or disease. The program also provides additional training in the musculoskeletal system, which will greatly enhance my knowledge base. As a prospective student, I am particularly attracted to UC-Davis's emphasis on the small-group, problem-based learning pathway, which allows students to reinforce the material that is presented in the classroom. By discussing and researching cases early in my medical school career, I will become a better doctor with more acute diagnostic skills.

As part of my program at UC-Davis, I plan to broaden my perspective by participating in an international clinical rotation. During a volunteer trip to Haiti after the 2010 earthquake, I gained a realistic view of medical care in an underserved area. Unfortunately, due to my limited health care experience, I did not have the knowledge or training to provide the residents with any meaningful treatment. In medical school, I will be better prepared to contribute to global humanitarian programs that serve disadvantaged communities. By sharing my skills, I can make a meaningful difference in an underserved area and become a more confident and experienced physician.

I am also attracted to the cultural diversity of California, where I eventually hope to practice. To serve the needs of this increasingly heterogeneous region, I must learn how to provide individualized care that honors each patient's cultural values. The program at UC-Davis is an integral part of my plan.

Finally, I feel a personal connection to the culture at UC-Davis that I have not experienced at other medical schools. After working in clinical settings and observing various patient interactions, I am convinced that a holistic philosophy is the best way to improve compliance and ensure a positive outcome. No program exemplifies these values and priorities better than UC-Davis.

<u>Our Assessment</u>: This essay conveys the candidate's fit for the program in a concise and effective way.

Why Our School

As an undergraduate student at Loma Linda University, I have enjoyed a challenging academic curriculum that emphasizes the values and teachings of the Seventh-day Adventist Church. Looking ahead, I am eager to attend a medical school that embodies similar spiritual ideals. Since 1866, Loma Linda University School of Medicine has upheld a principle that resonates strongly with me on a personal basis – that a doctor's mission is to use his body, mind, and soul to improve the lives of others. By integrating medicine with the values of the Seventh-day Adventist Church, Loma Linda offers a unique opportunity for students to define and understand their lifelong missions as healers.

As an active member of the Loma Linda community, I will share my knowledge and views with other like-minded students and faculty members. I am particularly eager to lend my skills to the Meridian Clinic, which provides educational and public health services for disadvantaged residents. By applying my classroom knowledge in a practical setting, I can embody the essence of generosity and service that the founding fathers held dear.

Loma Linda also offers the chance for me to conduct Independent Study in an area of personal interest. In recent months, I have worked as a researcher at the Loma Linda University Medical Center, where I am identifying the genetic risk factors for ovarian cancer. In medical school, I hope to continue this work under the direction of a mentor, such as Dr. Lisa Stanton in the Genetics Department. I am particularly intrigued by the work of Dr. Ronald Guzman at the Reagan Cancer Center, who is studying the role of nutrition in ovarian cancer angiogenesis. By lending my skills to this type of project, I can make a tangible contribution to an ongoing cancer investigation.

Finally, as a Colombian immigrant with extended family in Central and South America, I have a strong interest in different cultures and health care systems. During my final year of medical school, I plan to honor the church's tradition of serving others by participating in an international health care program that brings quality care to the people who need it the most.

By completing my education at Loma Linda, I will learn far more than medical theory and practice; I will gain critical insight into my role as a physician on a personal, professional, and spiritual basis. At this stage in my career, I am eager for the guidance, direction, and camaraderie that Loma Linda University School of Medicine will provide. No other program offers the chance to learn, grow, and contribute so much.

Our Assessment: For medical schools with a religious affiliation, students must demonstrate their commitment to the organization's ideals and goals. In this essay, this candidate fulfilled that objective in an extraordinary way.

Osteopathic Medicine

Throughout my nursing career, I have been deeply impressed by the physical and philosophical benefits of osteopathic techniques, which promote the body's natural ability to heal. From a clinical perspective, this proactive approach to medicine offers a rewarding opportunity to build connections with patients that focus on health, rather than illness. As a nursing student at the University of Maine, I was privileged to interact with several students in the osteopathic medicine program. Their positive impressions of their classes, faculty members, and career opportunities have convinced me that the University of Maine Osteopathic Medical School (UMOMS) will provide the rigorous, patient-centric education that I am seeking.

By design, UMOMS offers a nurturing faculty with a demonstrated commitment to underserved populations; it also attracts students who share this professional goal. Over the years, my personal physician, Dr. John Smith, has offered effusive praise for the training he received at UMOMS, including clinical rotations at prestigious local hospitals. If given a chance, I would be honored to complete my medical education in such a rigorous and vibrant community.

Compared to my peers, I will bring a wealth of experience and maturity to my studies at UMOMS. By working as a nurse in various clinical settings, I have gained a practical understanding of the challenges that physicians face to serve an increasingly diverse population. By volunteering at a free clinic, I have also become sensitive to the escalating cost of care, which prohibits the poorest and sickest patients from seeking timely intervention. Over time, I have acknowledged my desire to alleviate this critical gap in the health care system. As a nurse, I have a limited ability to help my patients improve their health. As an osteopathic physician, I can bring lasting change to an underserved community.

After medical school, I plan to open an osteopathic clinic in a poor or rural area, which offers a full range of preventive and primary care services. My goal is to provide the type of personalized, compassionate care that puts health before paperwork and patients before profits. By promoting the benefits of health education and preventive medicine, I can empower my patients to make positive choices that enhance their health and longevity. Eventually, I hope to mentor the next generation of osteopathic physicians, to preserve our profession's values and ideals. At UMOMS, I will acquire the knowledge, skills, and perspective I will need to achieve these goals and make a lasting difference in my community.

Our Assessment: This candidate was a successful nurse who was making the transition to a medical career. Her essay provided an eloquent discussion of her goals as an osteopathic physician, which were an excellent match for the program she chose.

Osteopathic Medicine

During my senior year of college, I spent my spring break on a volunteer trip to Haiti. For the first time, I saw the reality of medical care in a poor, underserved area. I spent two weeks conducting health surveys and handing out parasite medications to families outside Port a Prince. The children, who suffered from scabies, sores, and malnutrition, also shared a persistent respiratory infection. In my heart, I wished that I possessed the medical skills to make a meaningful difference in their lives.

When I returned to the United States, I was determined to gain additional experience in clinical medicine. During the summer of 2011, I worked as a medical assistant at a summer camp in rural West Virginia, where we served the needs of 80 energetic children. Throughout the course of the summer, we treated routine maladies such as scrapes, colds, poison ivy, buy bites, sprains, and bee stings. We also provided medication to children who had pre-existing conditions such as diabetes and asthma. Although my days at camp were long and tiring, they were also extremely satisfying.

Throughout the summer, I had the privilege of working closely with a highly skilled osteopathic physician. Dr. Wu didn't just treat the children's symptoms; he tried to determine the *cause* of their illness or injury. Then, he would help the child make appropriate changes to prevent a similar occurrence. Thanks to Dr. Wu, I discovered that an injury in one part of the body can affect many other parts. I also learned the implications of diet and exercise on everything from headaches to blood pressure. My challenging, but enjoyable, experiences at the camp confirmed my passion and proficiency for osteopathic medicine. After soothing the fears of dozens of feverish, homesick, bug bitten children, I knew that I had the temperament to succeed in this rigorous field.

When I returned to New York City, I accepted a position as a respiratory technician at Beth Israel Hospital, where I perform tests on patients in different departments. Within six months, I was promoted to the level of senior technician, which allows me to work closely with other members of the medical team. This additional experience has reinforced my commitment to the osteopathic philosophy, which takes a proactive approach to health care that increases a patients' well being and improves their compliance; it also encourages a stronger physician-patient bond.

Working with patients has taught me the importance of being realistic and flexible in my goals. Despite our best efforts, we cannot cure every illness or save every patient. Nevertheless, osteopathic physicians can provide hope and compassion during life's most difficult moments. They can also offer guidance, information, and support that traditional medicine does not provide. After medical school, I want to be the empathetic physician who provides my patients and their families with personalized service that suits their specific needs. By doing so, I can offer them their best chance for a happy and healthy future. For me, there is no greater or more worthy professional goal.

<u>Our Assessment</u>: This candidate had a wealth of medical experience, which made it difficult for her to decide which experiences to include in her statement. By focusing on her specific interest in the osteopathic philosophy, she delivered a focused essay that highlighted her reasons for choosing this specialty.

Osteopathic Medicine

When we first arrived in the United States, my parents could not afford the cost of my asthma treatments. To ease their burden, our family physician, Dr. Chen, offered to waive the fee for his services. Rather than accept this act of charity, my father suggested a bartering arrangement; in return for my treatment, he would clean the doctor's office building for a full year. This successful interaction taught me two lessons that continue to shape my life. From Dr. Chen, I learned that patients are a higher priority than profits. From my father, I learned the importance of giving back, regardless of my circumstances.

In subsequent years, I became attracted to the idea of becoming a physician like Dr. Chen, who uses his skills to help local families live longer and healthier lives. I was especially attracted to the benefits of osteopathic techniques, which teach patients how to minimize the onset of life-threatening illnesses by making the appropriate lifestyle choices. As a prospective physician, I am also attracted by the opportunity to form long-term relationships with my patients that focus on health and prevention, rather than disease.

For the past several years, I have shadowed Dr. Ling Li in her osteopathic practice in San Francisco. I have been consistently impressed by the compassionate and effective way that she treats her patients. Whenever possible, Dr. Li enhances the body's innate ability to heal. On one occasion, a patient suffered terrible headaches that resisted traditional treatment. By evaluating her habits and lifestyle, Dr. Li alleviated the frequency and intensity of the woman's headaches by suggesting a simple change in diet. Later, the patient confided to Dr. Li that no other physician had bothered to mention the implications of caffeine and alcohol, which were staples of her diet. I was impressed by the gentleness and simplicity of this solution, which offered immediate relief without expensive diagnostic tests or treatments.

By shadowing Dr. Li, I have witnessed the holistic and collaborative nature of the osteopathic approach. If she does not have an immediate solution to a patient's needs, Dr. Li consults with colleagues, reviews the latest research, and develops a customized treatment plan. By doing so, she is more than simply a doctor – she is a trusted friend and confidante who provides the education, information, and support that all patients deserve. Eventually, I hope to provide a comparable level of care in my own practice, to help my patients enjoy a better quality of life.

After working closely with DOs and MDs, I am convinced that osteopathic medicine is the best fit for my personality and goals. I enjoy forming close bonds with patients in a clinical setting, which are based on trust and respect. On a practical basis, I also want to promote a proactive approach to health care problems, to prevent the chance of recurrence. As an osteopathic physician, I can make the patient an equal partner in the healing process and offer specific guidelines to maximize health. This collaborative approach to medicine will yield better treatment plans and higher patient compliance.

Finally, by working in health care, I have become deeply sensitive to its high cost, which prohibits uninsured patients from seeking the services they need. Many times, while shadowing Dr. Li, I meet patients who cannot afford to fill their prescriptions. Other times, they take smaller doses of an essential drug to try to "stretch" their health care dollars. I am committed to alleviating these critical gaps in our current health care system. After I complete my medical degree, I plan to open an osteopathic practice in a poor or rural area. Through careful planning and management, I will become a trusted clinician who not only delivers babies, but serve their families' health care needs for a lifetime. I also hope to assume an educational role in my community by promoting the benefits of osteopathic techniques. With the training I receive at XXX, I can serve my patients in the same admirable manner as Drs. Chen and Li have served me.

Our Assessment: In this statement, the candidate eloquently describes his early interest in osteopathic medicine, which he continued to develop by shadowing Dr. Li. His insights into the profession, combined with his passion for the osteopathic philosophy, made a powerful impact on the committee.

Chapter 8: Addendums to Explain Unusual Situations

Ideally, in a perfect world, your grades and test scores will be an excellent fit for the medical school that you hope to attend. But what if they aren't? Many times, as part of their applications, candidates will attach a separate addendum to explain a disappointing grade or MCAT score. Their hope is that the explanation will compensate for a less than stellar "number" on their application. From our experience, these addendums rarely make a positive impact on the admissions committee.

Why? Most explanations are highly personal and difficult to verify. Other times, the excuse raises more questions than it actually answers, such as an announcement that the candidate does not perform well on standardized tests. Well, medical school will *require* you to pass dozens of timed tests in a highly competitive environment; if you cannot handle the MCAT, which is the only "constant" in the application process, how do you plan to pass your national boards? (I've yet to hear a persuasive answer to that question.)

Nevertheless, if you have a disappointing grade or MCAT score – and a legitimate explanation for it – you should definitely explain the situation to the admissions committee in the form of a short, well-written addendum. If possible, you should also have an objective third party (who has no vested interest in the admissions decision) document the situation in a persuasive recommendation letter.

What are legitimate explanations?

- Medical emergencies that can be documented by a physician's letter
- A serious illness or death in the immediate family
- Military commitments/relocations
- Work commitments necessitated by financial emergencies
- Your native language is not English
- You have a documented learning disability, but did not request special accommodations for the MCAT

In these cases, a well-written addendum that informs the committee of the situation (without making excuses) can greatly enhance your application. At the very least, it will give the reader some insight into the problems you have faced to complete your education and pursue your professional goals. This chapter contains several essays that candidates submitted to explain a disappointing GPA or MCAT score. We have also included addendums to explain other troublesome blemishes, such as an arrest record, job loss or a gap in your employment history.

To protect the privacy of the applicant, the names of all people, classes, schools, places, and companies have been changed.

Addendum to Explain Bad Grades

Although my recent academic performance is excellent, I wasn't always able to devote my complete energy to my school work. I was enrolled in the American International University during the collapse of the Colombian government, when the country underwent unprecedented economic turmoil and uncertainty. In a short period of time, my country experienced hyperinflation, rampant unemployment and a dramatic increase in violent crime. My family and I lost our life savings, including our family business. As a result, I found myself struggling to survive, rather than focusing on school.

Looking back, I am proud that I was able to balance my schoolwork with a full-time job at a restaurant. I did everything possible to ensure my family's survival during an extremely difficult time. Yet the stress of the economic overhaul made it impossible for me to concentrate on my studies. Many days, rather than prepare for exams, I stood in long lines to buy food. Thus, my grades from the American International University reflect the stress of these dire circumstances, rather than my actual ability.

Fortunately, they also show that I am a survivor. During a tumultuous situation, I was forced to re-evaluate my beliefs, aspirations and plans – and I simply refused to give up. Although my grades suffered, the experience clarified my goals, challenged my organizational skills and provided the strength I needed to overcome formidable obstacles. I am a survivor. What better strengths to bring to a medical career?

: This essay is short, focused, and sincere; it also contains information that can easily be verified by third-party sources. For one of his recommendations, this candidate submitted a letter from a professor in Colombia, who cited his extraordinary performance under pressure. The committee realized that he was an intelligent and hardworking young man who had done his best under difficult circumstances.

Addendum to Explain Bad Grades

When evaluating my application, I hope the committee will take into consideration my difficult adjustment to the United States. I moved to San Francisco at age fifteen, not knowing a word of English. My salvation was the school's bilingual education program, where I learned how to speak and write English, in addition to perfecting my fluency in Mandarin. With the tireless support of the faculty, I plunged into my new life in America, determined to embrace the many opportunities that were unavailable in my native Beijing.

Unfortunately, the language barrier prevented me from competing successfully with other students who were native speakers of English. Although I worked incredibly hard, my grades were primarily Bs and Cs, rather than the As I desired. Fortunately, as my English improved, so did my grades. By senior year, I was in the top 10% of my class, and won first place in the Westinghouse science competition. I was also elected as captain of Barrington High School's nationally acclaimed debate team.

Throughout my life, I have become deeply appreciative of the opportunities I have reaped by living in America. Yet my struggle to perfect the English language is most certainly reflected in my grades. With this in mind, I hope the committee will consider the tremendous challenges that my relocation required. In addition to learning a new language, I also had to adjust to a new culture and carve out a unique set of values and goals. This maturity will make me a more competent and empathetic physician.

Compared to other programs, XXX Medical School offers a solid academic reputation and a vibrant student body that celebrates cultural and socioeconomic diversity. I am eager to take my place on campus and make a positive contribution to the program. America has given me so much; I am eager to give back the fruits of my academic labor.

Our Assessment: This is a commendable essay from a candidate who had accomplished a great deal in a short period of time. By explaining the challenges she faced in a clear and sincere manner, she won the committee's full support.

Addendum to Explain Bad Grades

At age six, I was diagnosed with rheumatic fever, which required a level of medical intervention that was unavailable in my native Zambia. My diseased heart grew progressively worse and eventually interfered with my normal activities. Through the assistance of Doctors without Borders, I came to the United States for medical treatment in 1998. Although the American doctors successfully replaced my mitral valve, my adjustment to the American educational system proved to be as challenging as my medical problems. In addition to my poor English skills, I was unaccustomed to learning in a classroom setting. Throughout my childhood in Zambia, I had been sporadically tutored at home, but I had never attended school. Consequently, I found the formal education system in America to be physically and emotionally overwhelming.

Fortunately, I was up to the challenge. With the help of my adoptive family, I hired tutors in English, math and reading and quickly raised my grades to an acceptable level. During college, I maintained a 3.5 GPA, despite serious complications with my valve replacement. After working so hard to assimilate, I refused to let anything stop me from graduating with honors.

Although my GPA isn't the best, I cannot in good conscience blame my illness. After all, the same heart condition that nearly killed me also brought me to my wonderful new life in America. Through painful experience, I have learned to accept life's blessings along with its challenges. My illness forced me to become a more focused, patient, and resilient person who appreciates the value of every day. I also developed a tolerance for change, which, ironically, has been the one constant in my life. Although I have recovered from my childhood illness, I will retain its many lessons for the rest of my life.

<u>Our Assessment</u>: This essay offers an honest explanation of the candidate's struggles in the classroom. To document his time off from school, the candidate also submitted a letter from the surgeon who replaced his mitral valve. As a result, the committee understood the severity of the candidate's illness and recovery.

Addendum to Explain Bad Grades

My GPA was nearly perfect until I suffered a severe leg injury during my junior year of college. While driving home from my part-time job, I spun out of control on a patch of ice and injured my right leg. In that split second collision, I broke four bones and needed extensive surgery to repair them. I also needed physical therapy to rebuild the damaged tendons.

During my two months in rehab, my focus was on my own recovery rather than my schoolwork. Although I established a good rapport with my tutor, I couldn't concentrate on my assignments. During the first few weeks, I struggled with every minor detail of my hospitalization. I went from being a confident student to a helpless patient who needed help to go to the bathroom. Thanks to the exceptional doctors, nurses and counselors on staff, I managed to get past my initial anger and complete my rehab in just nine weeks.

Unfortunately, the emotional effects of the accident lingered well into my senior year. Because of the residual damage to my leg, I could no longer play football, which had been a huge source of enjoyment and pride. My concentration deficit was also troubling. During the fall semester, I struggled with a heavy course load, including advanced classes in Statics and Electricity. Rather than take a reduced load, I opted to simply do my best and hope that my concentration would improve. Although it eventually did, my GPA paid a heavy price. I hope the admissions committee will understand.

Two professors (Drs. Davis and Hanson), along with my rehab specialist (Dr. White), have provided reference letters to document my struggles after the accident. I offer their letters not as an excuse, but as evidence of the powerful support that I needed to regain my mobility and graduate on time. Several friends and advisors suggested that I take a year off to fully recover. Looking back, that option probably would have enabled me to get better grades, but I am proud to be able to graduate as originally scheduled. The accident was a setback, but not a fatal one. If given a chance, I will bring my dedication and tenacity to all of my endeavors in medical school. I am "back in the game" and ready to show you what I can do.

<u>Our Assessment</u>: This candidate shows the reader the *right* way to document an accident that caused a drop in GPA. He told the story quickly and honestly, including his controversial decision to accelerate his workload in order to graduate with his class. Most importantly, he included letters from two faculty members and a physician, who documented his situation in a supportive way. As a result, the committee understood the obstacles the candidate faced to complete his classes and recover from his injuries.

Addendum to Explain a Low GPA

During my junior year of college, my father lost his job as an accountant for United Airlines. Although my mother continued to work as a retail clerk, her salary was not enough to cover our basic living expenses. Within a few months, my parents depleted their savings during my father's unsuccessful job search. Without a miracle, we faced the frightening possibility of losing our family home.

Despite my heavy academic load, I accepted a position as a web designer at Brevard Community College to supplement my mother's income. Balancing a 30-hour work week with a full-time course load was a difficult challenge that left me exhausted and overwhelmed. Sadly, it also diminished my formerly perfect GPA. Despite my best efforts, I did not obtain top grades in my math and science classes, which required considerable outside preparation. On several occasions, I missed our weekly study sessions in order to work enough hours to pay our monthly bills. As a result, my greatest accomplishment is not completing my education, but keeping my family safe and united during this crisis.

My journey, although stressful, has given me the confidence and stamina to pursue my passion for medicine. After tackling this enormous responsibility in a positive manner, I am certain that I can handle the challenges that medical school will bring.

<u>Our Assessment</u>: In this short essay, the candidate proved to the committee that he was a survivor. During a tough time, he did what was necessary to help his family and complete his education. By balancing these

demands, he developed practical skills that will enhance his performance in medical school.

Addendum to Explain a Low MCAT Score

Despite my best efforts, I have been unable to achieve the exceptional MCAT scores that are expected at a school of Brown's caliber. Over the Christmas holidays, I took an extensive MCAT prep course, along with private tutoring sessions with a faculty member. Even with personal coaching, I have been unable to exceed a cumulative score of 25. I am frustrated by these results, because they do not reflect the academic excellence that I have consistently displayed in the classroom.

Despite my difficulty with the MCAT, I am convinced that I am an excellent candidate for your program. Over the past decade, I have developed myriad practical skills that cannot be assessed by standardized testing. I am fluent in four languages and a successful violinist in a professional orchestra. Between 2005 and 2008, I traveled all over the world with the Vienna Boys Choir. Clearly, my MCAT scores do not accurately reflect my fluency in English, proficiency in music, or my unique multi-cultural experiences.

Although I respect your use of the MCAT as a screening tool, I hope that you will consider the "full picture" of my academic, professional and cross-cultural training in making your final admissions decision. I have worked very hard to achieve aggressive professional goals, and I will bring a wealth of practical experience to the classroom. If given the opportunity, I will be a tremendous asset to your program.

<u>Our Assessment</u>: Many students write addendums to explain a disappointing MCAT score. Few have done it better than this candidate, who explained: (1) the efforts he made to obtain a top score and (2) the distinctive strengths that he would bring to medical school.

The only controversial part of the essay is his decision to mention his preparation for the MCAT, which included an expensive course and one-on-one tutoring. On one hand, this clearly suggests that the candidate took the test seriously and did whatever he could to prepare for it. On the other hand, it also shows that he had significant financial resources, which some schools consider to be an unfair advantage.

Thankfully, in this case, the candidate's application was otherwise strong, which made the MCAT tutoring and prep course a non-issue. But, from our perspective, this is something that candidates should consider before they disclose that they took an expensive MCAT course. It definitely shows initiative, but it also shows that you have more money than other applicants (who scored well *without* an expensive course). Consequently, it may invite a level of scrutiny that you did not expect.

Addendum to Explain a Low MCAT Score

Like many foreigners who were raised in the United States, I often felt like a fish out of water. My parents moved to the US when I was 14, which subjected me to a huge cultural change that would subsequently define my childhood. My hardest adjustments were with language. Nothing was as difficult as having to learn English with little academic support. The school department in Raleigh had no ESL facilities, so I learned English by working with an old set of Berlitz tapes. It was not easy. My initial attempts at conversation were particularly frustrating. I could visually "see" the word in my mind, but I could not verbalize it. Verb conjugation was a nightmare (sing, sang, sung) as were similar sounding words (to, two, too). Throughout high school and college, mastering English has been my greatest challenge.

Although I have excelled in my coursework, I still have serious difficulties with the language portion of most standardized tests. Consequently, my performance on the verbal portion of the MCAT is not nearly as high as I had hoped. To compensate for this deficiency, I continue to take elective classes in speech and writing; I also volunteer as a language tutor for new students from South America.

As an aspiring physician, I want to express myself with confidence, both verbally and in writing. I look forward to developing these skills in medical school, where I will embrace every opportunity to write papers and speak in front of an audience. I am certain that I will succeed. While navigating the difficult transition from Costa Rica to the US, I developed the confidence to weather even the hardest storms.

<u>Our Assessment</u>: This candidate essentially learned English on her own, which her school principal confirmed in his recommendation letter. As a result, the committee understood the terrible hurdle the candidate faced to score well on standardized tests.

Addendum to Explain a Low MCAT Score

In the spring of 2009, I prepared diligently for the April MCAT, knowing that the results would play a major role in determining where I would obtain my medical education. After months of drills, mock tests and classroom preparation, I was ready to show the Admissions Committee that I could conquer this marathon exam.

Six days before the test, I was rushed to the emergency room at Southland Community Hospital with the most excruciating pain of my life. Lab results showed an inflamed appendix that required immediate removal. Following surgery on April 1 (see attached note from my attending physician), I recovered at the hospital for three days and returned home on Thursday, April 5. Considering my four-inch incision, my doctor recommended complete bed rest for at least five weeks.

With the MCAT scheduled for April 7, I found myself in an unenviable position. Although my surgery was certainly a valid reason for missing the exam, the April testing date was the last one to qualify for 2009 admission. If I missed the April test, my medical education would have been delayed by an entire year. At the time, it seemed like an eternity.

Determined to enroll in medical school in the fall of 2010, I refused to miss that test. Against everyone's advice, my brother drove me to the testing site on Saturday morning and waited for me nervously in the car. I could barely stand up, much less concentrate on complex reasoning problems. Nevertheless, I survived the test and even skipped my prescription painkillers that afternoon. I was hurting, exhausted and sore beyond belief, but I completed the test. My final score (XX) is respectable, but certainly not what I expected.

As I complete my application, I am fully recovered from my surgery and eager to begin my medical training. Yet my low MCAT score haunts me, not just because of its mediocrity, but because of the unusual circumstances that surround it. Throughout my college career, I have worked diligently to distinguish myself as a versatile candidate who is highly suited for the medical profession. My grades, work experiences and personal references all support my honorable intentions and goals. Clearly, my MCAT score does not reflect my academic potential, but the extenuating circumstances I faced on the testing day. I hope the committee will consider this as a mitigating factor when they make their admissions decision.

Our Assessment: This candidate told the entire story behind his disappointing MCAT score, which was supported by letters from his physicians. As a result, the committee understood that his score did not reflect his true ability to succeed in medical school.

Addendum to Explain a Low MCAT Score

In high school and college, I attained a 3.9 GPA without requesting special accommodations for my learning disabilities (dyslexia and ADHD). By employing effective study techniques, I achieved excellent grades under the same testing conditions as my peers. For philosophical reasons, I chose not to inform my professors or academic advisors of my "special needs" or challenges. Instead, I opted to keep the focus on my talents, rather than my limitations.

Few people supported my position, including my parents and family doctor. In fact, they unanimously agreed that my efforts to compete with "normal" students were doomed to fail. As you might expect, my decision ultimately provided a wonderful sense of empowerment. By thriving academically, I confirmed my ability to succeed in difficult situations, which inspired my commitment to other aspects of personal growth. Contrary to what my guidance counselor told me, there isn't anything I can't do.

In the same vein, I am proud of my "average" MCAT scores, which I also achieved without special testing accommodations. Although it may not seem particularly impressive, it proves that I can perform at parity with other candidates under extremely stressful circumstances. And to me, that is paramount. After graduation, I will be expected to demonstrate the same skills as my peers. Why not start now?

Our Assessment: For personal reasons, this candidate did not request special accommodations in the classroom or for the MCAT. In this essay, he not only explains that choice, but shows the reader the confident and inspirational person that he is. The essay was well perceived.

Addendum to Explain a Gap in Employment or Education

My parents divorced during my freshman year of high school, which left my mother as the sole support of three small children. As the oldest, I felt a strong responsibility to help her. Just fourteen years old, I got a job as a waitress in a neighborhood diner and contributed my earnings to the household. Between school and work, my schedule left little time for homework, hobbies or extracurricular activities. After a year with virtually no sleep, I realized that I could no longer continue to juggle so many responsibilities.

Sadly, my family's needs had to come first. After withdrawing from high school, I worked full-time at the diner, along with a second job at Variety Print Shop. I took evening classes to prepare for the GED exam, which I passed in October of 2004. After seven long years of night classes, I finally completed my BA in Psychology at the University of Massachusetts-Amherst in 2010. No victory was ever as sweet as walking across the stage to receive my diploma!

As I complete my application for medical school, I am painfully aware of how different I am from your traditional applicants. I have nothing to discuss in the sections of the application that ask about hobbies, sports or campus affiliations. My priority was always providing for my family and completing my education; I rarely had the luxury to dream, to follow my passions, or to consider "what if." Compared to more financially secure candidates, I probably sound like a "charity case."

But I prefer the term "winner." At first glance, I haven't had much of an opportunity to demonstrate key leadership skills, yet I have certainly succeeded at building my own life. I persevered in situations in which most people would have given up. I found solutions to difficult problems that seemingly had no answers. I provided for my siblings, to ensure that they would have the chance to find their own success and pursue their own dreams. And I never, EVER complained about the hand that life dealt me, either financially or socially. I am, after all, a self-made woman with the power to transcend seemingly insurmountable challenges. Isn't that what superior leadership is all about?

Our Assessment: This essay is masterful, both in its content and simplicity. The reader clearly understands what the candidate has overcome to complete her education and pursue her dreams.

Addendum to Explain a Gap in Employment or Education

After five years of marriage, I gave birth to my daughter Emily in 2006. Originally, I intended to return to my position at Quaker Oats, Inc., but I had a last minute change of heart. Acknowledging the importance of my baby's first year, I opted to be a stay-at-home mom. Thankfully, my husband's income as a prosecutor was enough to cover our expenses for my one-year sabbatical.

During my time off, I discovered the need for a pregnancy resource center for other young women in the Warren area. Located sixty miles from the nearest major city (San Francisco), local mothers lacked convenient access to counseling, well-baby care, infant and toddler play groups and basic lactation support. I started Madonna & Child Ltd. to address these needs.

Our program provides free and low cost services to all mothers in the Warren/ Barrington area. I raised awareness for the program by making presentations at high schools, college campuses and women's groups in the city. I also solicited donations from local businesses, which were generous with their time, expertise and money. After a slow start, Madonna & Child Ltd. developed a great reputation around the city. After four years of continuous growth, we now have 46 volunteers and over 500 new mothers participating in the program. We provide a comprehensive array of services (GED classes, instruction in baby care, nutrition classes, job hunting skills, and anger management classes) in a supportive, non-judgmental environment.

Although I started Madonna & Child Ltd. as a volunteer resource, it soon became my professional calling. My commitment to the group enables me to enrich the lives of mothers and children in a unique manner. Since 2007, I have served as the company's president and CEO, which requires me to oversee all aspects of the organization's administration and management. After medical school, I plan to pursue similar opportunities in the public sector.

Our Assessment: This essay not only explains the candidate's gap in employment, but the unique contribution she has made to her community through the non-profit organization that she launched. It was as persuasive and well-written as her primary statement.

Addendum to Explain a Gap in Employment or Education

Following my junior year of college, I took a one-year sabbatical to assist with a critical public health crisis in my native South Africa. After a three-day riot destroyed Cape Town's impoverished Zenatta Hospital, the government requested that all available medical personnel report for duty. As a licensed practical nurse with Medivac experience, my services were in particularly high demand.

Between August of 2009 and July of 2010, I worked nearly eighty hours per week in the Cape Town facility. Because most of the surgical theatres had been destroyed by the riots, I often assisted with surgeries in temporary facilities. Doctors postponed all elective and non-critical procedures, yet we were still overwhelmed by the need for medicine, caregivers and preventive health measures. With few practicing physicians in the community, our emergency room was the only available health care resource.

Throughout my year at the hospital, I heard disparate reports about the causes of the nation's national health crisis. The staff reported widespread misuse of funds, while the national newspaper accused the government of abusing international aid. Whatever the root causes, I found myself in the untenable position of losing patients to potentially curable illnesses because of a lack of money and pharmaceuticals. Sadly, government corruption and media restrictions prevented public appreciation of the issues or the implementation of effective remedies. I was frustrated by my inability to improve the situation.

I returned to college in August of 2010 with a profound skepticism regarding the future of South Africa, which is plagued by secrecy and corruption. Yet, my hopelessness with my country is occasionally replaced by a newfound confidence. With a strong educated response, along with the skills I will gain from studying in the US, I am confident that I will make meaningful changes in the administration of health care, medical charities and other public aid funds in South Africa.

Our Assessment: This statement is from an older candidate who went back to school to complete her pre-medical requirements after working for several years as a licensed practical nurse. Her detailed account of her emergency sabbatical gives the reader keen insight into her maturity, motivation, and perseverance under difficult circumstances.

Addendum to Explain a Gap in Employment or Education

In the spring semester of my sophomore year at Sarah Lawrence College, my brother died of AIDS. Chris had contracted the disease five years earlier from a tainted unit of blood that he received during emergency surgery. Although my family had known of his diagnosis for years, we were emotionally unprepared for his death. Unable to return to college after Chris's funeral, I wound up taking two years off.

If left to my own devices, I probably would have moped in my room for most of that time. Fortunately, Chris's friends had other ideas. Within a week of his death, his best friend from the local AIDS hospice asked me to participate in a new program designed to promote AIDS awareness in the community. At the first meeting, I realized immediately how much I was needed. The other advocacy groups in town were largely ceremonial in nature; they organized fundraisers, solicited donations and provided financial support for uninsured patients. However, no one was working on the most urgent need, which was education.

I became the official liaison between the group and the local high schools, where we presented free seminars on AIDS prevention. Our first classes were somewhat awkward because I could not discuss sex without embarrassment, but the message was so powerful and important that I never lost my focus. In fact, my youthfulness definitely worked in my favor. At the end of my talks, the kids asked relevant questions about how to "stay safe" in both casual and committed relationships. They helped me to see that I had valuable information to share, even if the topics were intimate and embarrassing.

After returning to Sarah Lawrence in 2009, I continued to teach classes and train new participants in the program. During the past year, I have given speeches on AIDS awareness to both the regional and national Sigma Tau sorority conferences. Four years after losing Chris, I feel closer to him than ever. I think he would be proud of my work to prevent others from suffering from HIV. My commitment to educating teens is his legacy to me, which I am honored to share with anyone who will listen. With education and awareness, we *will* win this fight.

<u>Our Assessment</u>: The honesty and eloquence of this essay made it far more than simply an "explanation" for the candidate's educational gap. It showed the reader the impact of her brother's death, which inspired her to help prevent the spread of HIV/AIDS in children. After reading it, the committee knew how generous, special, and effective a person she truly was.

Addendum to Explain Arrest / Criminal History

On March 15, 2008, I drove three friends home from our spring break vacation in Daytona Beach, Florida. After nine grueling hours, I didn't realize the magnitude of my fatigue. When I reached the Ohio border, I encountered the worst snowstorm I had ever seen. Although I was tempted to stop at a rest area, I didn't want to delay our arrival. Against my better judgment, I continued driving.

Less than an hour later, I hit a patch of ice and crossed the center line of Route 55, where I hit the driver's side of a Federal Express delivery truck. Fortunately, since both vehicles were traveling at reduced speeds, there were no injuries (other than emotional trauma). Unfortunately, my bad decision had immediate legal repercussions. The Ohio State Trooper cited me for hazardous driving and for failure to maintain control of my vehicle. Three months later, I plead *nolo contendere* at my court appearance in Columbus, Ohio. I received a $500 fine and was ordered to complete a driver education class.

Looking back, I am extremely embarrassed by the incident and my poor judgment. While trying to appear "cool," I caused a horrible accident that jeopardized five young lives. Since that day, I have been an exceptional driver who is reluctant to take chances. The accident gave me an increased appreciation for the long-term effects of bad driving. I will never make a similar mistake again.

<u>Our Assessment</u>: This essay is short, focused, and sincere. The author also attached a short note from the teacher of his driver education course, who vouched for his maturity and character. As a result, the committee recognized that the incident was not a character defect, but a regrettable error in judgment.

Addendum to Explain Arrest / Criminal History

Two months into my internship with Zenith Computer, the company opted to outsource the manufacturing of our mother boards to a tiny firm in Korea. Although senior management assured us that the company was not a sweatshop that used child labor, I had my doubts. In my previous internship with Wyatt Computer, I had visited a manufacturing plant in the same Korean city where Zenith planned to do business. I saw with my own eyes the age of the workers and the inhumane conditions that they endured. I strongly disagreed with Zenith's decision to support this practice.

Although I was not in a position to change the decision, I presented a videotape of my footage from Korea to a sympathetic manager in human resources. She promised to show it to the senior manager who was in charge of the move. She also asked me to document my concerns in a memo. Unfortunately, my efforts did not alter the firm's decision to outsource the manufacturing function. In late 2007, they proceeded with the move to Korea.

Six months later, when the child labor issue became public knowledge, I led an organized demonstration outside Zenith's Los Angeles headquarters. I was no longer an employee of the firm, simply a concerned citizen who was trying to raise awareness for an atrocious issue. When we refused to voluntarily end our demonstration, Zenith's security team called the Los Angeles Police Department and we were all arrested for disturbing the peace. The charges were eventually dropped when Zenith's legal team failed to appear at a required hearing.

Looking back, I have mixed emotions about leading the demonstration. On one hand, I was honored to publicly challenge a cause as despicable as child labor. On the other hand, a criminal conviction could have handicapped my goal of becoming a physician, which would have been devastating to me. Since then, I have pursued less stressful and controversial ways to draw attention to this issue, such as blogging, which I was not aware of during my internship. By doing so, I can support this cause without disrupting my own professional future.

<u>Our Assessment</u>: In this essay, the candidate explained his decision to support an admirable cause in a less than admirable way. The committee was impressed by his passion, honesty, and willingness to put his freedom on the line for his ideals. More importantly, they respected his subsequent decision to support the

cause in more honorable ways, which would prevent the risk of being arrested in the future.

Addendum to Explain Arrest / Criminal History

While driving home from Atlanta's 2006 Fourth of July Parade, I was pulled over during a random DUI screening. Unfortunately, my blood alcohol level was 0.014, which was slightly over the legal limit. I was charged with underage drinking and driving under the influence and was released on my own recognizance. Rather than face the expense of a trial, I plead guilty to the charges in October of 2007. I lost my license for six months, paid a $1500 fine and completed a court-ordered program in drug and alcohol awareness.

During my mandatory classes, I was impressed by the speakers from Students Against Drunk Driving (SADD), including two of my fellow students from UGA. Their frank discussions about alcohol abuse and its devastating effects forced me to reconsider my own personal habits. In my first year of college, I often drank five or six beers on a weekend night and got into my car to drive home. It never occurred to me that I was breaking the law or that my actions could hurt someone else. Although I considered myself a responsible driver, my DUI suggested otherwise.

To my surprise, the speakers were all "nice kids" who had made tragic mistakes while drinking and driving. One girl had caused an accident that killed a young child. After hearing their stories, I realized how foolish and misguided my actions had been. I promised myself that I would never drink and drive again.

After I completed my mandatory classes in drug and alcohol awareness, I joined the UGA chapter of SADD. Two years later, I remain one of its most committed members. By volunteering as a designated driver, I am determined to doing my part to prevent drunk driving.

Our Assessment: This essay explains an unfortunate mistake that many students make- they drink and drive, which can have deadly consequences. In this case, the candidate's record was expunged after he completed his court-ordered drug awareness program. Otherwise, the charges would have remained on his record and prevented him from gaining admission to medical school. Along with this addendum, the candidate submitted the actual court record, along with a letter from the judge that stated that he had satisfied all of the terms of his plea agreement. Thankfully, the medical school accepted his explanation and granted him admission to their program. Normally, they do not overlook this sort of discretion.

Addendum to Explain Arrest / Criminal History

On my seventeenth birthday, my boyfriend invited me to dinner and a movie at our local shopping mall. While we waited for the show to begin, we took a casual walk through the neighboring stores. Unbeknownst to me, my boyfriend slipped an expensive watch into his pocket while we browsed through a small jewelry shop. When we tried to leave, the security tag on the watch triggered the alarm system and we were immediately surrounded by security guards. We spent the next two hours at the police station, answering some very embarrassing questions.

Although I did not know about the watch, we were both charged with shoplifting and were released to our parents' custody. Ultimately, the store agreed to drop the charges if we would pay for the watch. Needless to say, we apologized profusely to the store manager and paid full retail value for the timepiece.

Although the charges may not appear on my criminal record, the experience changed my life. I faced an evening in jail, along with the embarrassment of having to call my parents. I will never forget the look of shame and disappointment on my mother's face. After spending a lifetime teaching me right from wrong, she never thought that I would steal – or date someone who would. I let her down. I also lost respect for my boyfriend, who was clearly not the honest person I thought he was.

The incident taught me a powerful lesson about the importance of character. Since then, I have been extremely selective in who I choose to befriend. At the same time, I faced the formidable challenge of earning back the respect of my own family. Fortunately, over time, my parents acknowledged that my mistake was not being a thief, but trusting the wrong person. We have subsequently worked very hard to heal as a family.

Our Assessment: In reality, this candidate did not have to disclose this incident, because no charges were filed against her. Nevertheless, the committee respected her for being honest enough to reveal it to them and explain its impact on her life. As part of her application, the candidate reinforced this positive impression by submitting strong recommendation letters that confirmed her personal character.

Addendum to Explain Arrest / Criminal History

On October 11, 1999, I was pulled over by the police and charged with improper lane usage. While inspecting the car, the police found 8 oz. of cannabis, which resulted in an additional charge for possession. On December 1, 1999, the cannabis charge was suppressed; the final disposition was "Motion state stricken on leave to reinstate." On January 4, 2000, I received supervision and a $50 fine for the traffic violation. The case is logged under San Diego Police Dept. - Complaint #9618-93.

Ten years later, I am still embarrassed and humbled by this experience. At age nineteen, I made the mistake of experimenting with something that was illegal and dangerous. I do not use drugs today, nor do I condone their use by others. I deeply regret the pain and embarrassment that my mistake caused my family.

In hindsight, I wish that I had possessed the maturity and insight to have made a better decision. Unfortunately, I made an error in judgment. When evaluating my application, I hope that the committee will consider this incident as an aberration in my otherwise happy, healthy, successful thirty-year life. It was a regrettable mistake that does not in any way reflect the maturity and integrity I will bring to your program.

Our Assessment: This author did an excellent job of documenting the incident and apologizing for it. The committee was impressed by his ability to put the incident behind him and live a healthy and drug-free life. Nevertheless, the candidate's acceptance was not a unanimous decision; one committee member voted against him, due to his own zero-tolerance policy regarding drug use.

Addendum to Explain a Job Loss

In 2007, I became the General Manager for Tropical Gardens, which is a $25 million dollar natural produce business that supplies fresh fruit and organic vegetables to restaurants and food service institutions in northern California. Later that year, I became engaged to the owner's daughter, who coordinated the firm's public relations work. For nearly three years, we worked together in a family business that we hoped to eventually pass on to our children.

Everything changed in the spring of 2010, when my fiancé had second thoughts about our impending marriage. Over a period of three weeks, her "uncertainty" morphed into a realization that she preferred to sever our relationship. I later discovered that her reservations were due to her budding relationship with one of our suppliers. Rather than lead me on, she opted to defer our marriage plans in order to explore another romantic relationship. Needless to say, I was personally and professionally crushed.

To his credit, my fiance's father, who was the president of our firm, never took sides or demanded my resignation. In fact, he continually praised me for doing a commendable job under increasingly stressful circumstances. Nevertheless, I found it impossible to ignore the strained relationships in the office. Eventually, I concluded that such a small company could not thrive if we tried to co-exist together. With mixed emotions, I submitted my resignation in August of 2010 and stayed onboard long enough to train my replacement. Fortunately, a few months later, I located a similar position with Sunkist Foods in San Francisco.

I am grateful for my professional success at Tropical Gardens and for the mature way in which I handled a difficult situation. Sadly, I also learned a painful lesson in not mixing business with pleasure. Whatever the future holds, I will think long and hard before I become romantically involved with a colleague. After my experience at Tropical Gardens, I am extremely reluctant to risk losing another excellent job to the whims of romance.

Our Assessment: Many people find themselves in the same position as this candidate, which forces them to make a difficult professional choice for personal reasons. This essay documented his career transition in a professional and articulate way.

Addendum to Explain a Job Loss

Following my graduation from Columbia University, I accepted a position teaching high school English at a small Baptist school in northern Mississippi. The job was an excellent fit for my degree in education and a unique opportunity to live in a close-knit rural community.

Unfortunately, my liberal religious beliefs were a poor fit for the conservative local diocese. On a regular basis, I received negative feedback for my decision to discuss current events from a secular perspective. From the administration's view, my job was to present the Christian position on each topic and to label all non-Christian influences as negative or destructive. If a student questioned that perspective or asked for my opinion, I was advised to refer them to the Bible. No additional discussion would be permitted.

By the end of my first semester, I felt that I was in an untenable position. The restrictions that were placed on my classroom discussions not only stifled my enjoyment of the job, but my students' ability to learn. By the Christmas holiday season, I felt trapped in my increasingly inhospitable environment. In early spring, the principal informed me that the diocese would not renew my contract for the following school year. Although I hated being fired, I knew that continuing in the job would have been a poor choice for everyone.

Looking back, I accepted the job for all the wrong reasons, without considering the poor interpersonal "fit." As an open-minded woman, I was appalled by the school's inflexible position on topics of moral and social relevance. In my mind, my job was to encourage discussion and nurture independent thinking, not to simply parrot the school's "party line." Fortunately, I quickly landed another teaching position at a public school outside Biloxi. My employers not only tolerated, but supported, my commitment to lively classroom discussions. In fact, I was named "Teacher of the Year" in the Biloxi school district for five consecutive years.

Our Assessment: This candidate did an excellent job of explaining her poor fit for the religious culture at the school where she worked. By writing this essay, she showed considerable insight into her own personality and values, which highly impressed the committee. She also had the opportunity to tell "her side" of a difficult professional situation that one of her recommendation letters also addressed.

Addendum to Explain a Job Loss

I was fired from my position as quality control director for Tommy Hilfiger Ltd. when I defied my supervisor's order to substitute a lower quality fabric for a top retailer. Although the unethical substitution would have saved us nearly six million dollars, it was a clear violation of our original agreement with the buyer. Worse, the difference in quality was noticeable enough to potentially damage our reputation in the marketplace. I refused to go along with the ruse.

Although I was comfortable with my decision to honor my conscience, being a "whistleblower" cost me my job. My boss, who ruled by intimidation and fear, denied my claims and blamed me for the "miscommunication." Considering the disparity in our positions, senior management chose to support my boss. After a brief meeting, I was ordered to vacate the building by the end of the day.

This experience challenged everything I previously understood about teamwork, honesty and doing my best for my company. When senior management refused to back me, I felt that several of my sacred values had been defiled. Sadly, despite his technical strengths, my boss was willing to risk the long-term loss of our brand to achieve a short-term gain. Fortunately, he was fired from the company within a year of the incident, which validated my decision to report his deception. I later discovered that he had made similar substitutions in the past, but that I was the first person to stand up to him. Word of my "insubordination" had slowly trickled into the executive suite and prompted closer scrutiny of the tyrant's unethical practices.

Although my supervisor's undoing came too late to salvage my career at Tommy Hilfiger, it confirmed my commitment to honesty in all aspects of business. Regardless of the temptation to cheat or take shortcuts, I will only be successful if I am willing to be ethically correct and fully accountable for my actions. For the rest of my career, I am determined to be the antithesis of my unethical former boss.

Our Assessment: This candidate paid a heavy price for adhering to her convictions. Nevertheless, she made a positive impression on the admissions committee, who respected her maturity and integrity in a difficult situation.

Addendum to Explain a Job Loss

As an Arab-American woman, I lived for nearly twelve years in the United States without enduring a single act of discrimination. Everything changed after September 11, when fear and mistrust permeated the XXX campus, where I was a Teaching Assistant in two classes in International Relations. In the aftermath of the attacks, I was taunted by profanity and various acts of aggression. One student, with whom I had enjoyed an excellent rapport, actually told me to "burn in hell" when I tried to defend the Muslim religion.

Needless to say, I was horrified by the hostility that was directed toward my Arab friends, students and peers. As a Teaching Assistant at the university, I hoped to do my part to confront this anger and prevent other people from being victimized. Unfortunately, my efforts could not stop the misdirected hostility of shell-shocked students. For several weeks, I questioned my decision to remain in the United States.

The point became moot by December, when the department opted not to renew my teaching stipend for the following semester. The dean insisted that my performance was not the issue; rather, the situation was a direct result of "decreased interest" in International Relations and Policy classes on campus. Considering the immediate need for soldiers and government workers with a cultural understanding of the Arabic culture and languages, I considered the administration's explanation to be disingenuous. Unfortunately, as an undergraduate student, I was in no position to protect my job.

Ironically, losing my stipend gave me a once-in-a-lifetime chance to serve my country. In January of 2002, I accepted an internship to teach Arabic at the American embassy in Jordan. I was honored to educate others about my native language and culture, and to provide a friendly face during a stressful time. Thankfully, my reception in Jordan was significantly friendlier than that on the XXX campus. My students understood that patriots come in all races and wear all styles of clothing. Although I am proud of my Arab heritage, I love being an American and I am committed to preventing further acts of terrorism. I am honored to serve my country in any way possible.

Throughout my year in Jordan, I re-committed myself to a medical career and recovered from the shock of the discrimination I faced in America. When I returned to the United States, I embraced my future with an optimism and clarity I never dreamed possible. As I plan my future and set new goals, I am proud to have made a difference in my own unique way. It was my honor and responsibility as an American.

Our Assessment: This addendum is powerful and eloquent enough to serve as a diversity statement. To the committee, it was a sad reminder of the personal losses that people experienced in the aftermath of September 11, when the emotions of grief-stricken survivors occasionally clouded their judgment.

Chapter 9: A Second Chance: Responses to Waitlist Notices

Contrary to conventional wisdom, getting into medical school isn't a simple "yes or no" proposition. In reality, there are three possible responses to your application: acceptance, rejection or waitlisting. The third category is a frustrating limbo into which thousands of candidates fall each year. What does it mean if you are placed on a waitlist for a top tier medical school?

On the positive side, receiving a waitlist letter means that you have qualified for admission. The committee evaluated your application and confirmed that your background and experience were a good fit for their program. But here's where it gets sticky; although they didn't say "no" to your request for admission, they didn't say "yes," either.

Unfortunately, top schools will rarely reveal why a particular candidate is on the waitlist or what (s)he can do to improve his/her chances. Nevertheless, if you are waitlisted at your absolute first-choice school, you have nothing to lose by continuing to market yourself to the Admissions Committee. Unless the school discourages additional contact, we recommend that you take a pro-active approach. Send a letter that restates your interest in the program. Explain the unique contribution that you will make if they admit you.

Keep the letter short and sweet -- two pages maximum. Resist the urge to summarize your life history; instead, stay focused on what you have accomplished since you first applied. Also resist the urge to discuss your disappointment at not being accepted. Your tone must be upbeat and gracious.

This chapter contains three essays/letters that candidates submitted in response to being waitlisted. To protect the privacy of the applicant, the names of all people, classes, schools, places, and companies have been changed.

Medical School Waitlist Letter

Please accept this letter as my heartfelt intention to remain on the waitlist for admission to Georgetown University Medical School. My recent work as a researcher and clinician has solidified my commitment to the profession and has helped me to better define my long-term goals. Consequently, I am certain that Georgetown is the best possible fit for my talents and aspirations.

New Accomplishments. Since I originally applied to medical school last summer, I have completed my BS in Chemistry at Harvard University with a perfect 4.0 GPA. In addition to my academic success, I also invested considerable time in several outside activities to prepare for medical school:

1. While shadowing physicians at Harvard Medical School, I observed angiograms and angioplasties at the cardiac catheter lab, shadowed an attending in the telemetry unit, and learned about the administration and interpretation of echocardiograms from a third-year cardiology fellow. My most memorable experience was visiting cardiology outpatients with Dr. Alicia Sone, an assistant professor of medicine at Harvard. Her warm bedside manner and graceful handling of difficult patients taught me the importance of compassion in patient care.

2. Since August of 2010, I have served as the volunteer coordinator for the American Medical Students Association (AMSA) at Harvard, where I have organized membership campaigns, promotional activities and community outreach programs in the greater Boston area. In early 2012, I chaired a campus fundraiser that raised $20,000 for cancer research.

3. In December of 2010, my father was diagnosed with Gaucher Disease, which is a progressive and debilitating genetic disorder with limited treatment options. While assisting with his care, I gained a profound appreciation of a life-threatening disease from the patient's perspective. My role in my father's treatment and recovery encompasses several diverse aspects of the health care profession; on any given day, I am a nurse, social worker, friendly visitor and genetic researcher.

My father's disease inspired not only my undergraduate research, but my long-term goal as a physician. For my independent study project, I investigated novel methods to diagnose and treat Gaucher Disease. During the past year, I have met several patients who are struggling with the same fears and challenges as my father. I cherish their willingness to share the most private and frightening aspects of their lives just to help my research. By facing a debilitating illness with courage and grace, they have taught me the importance of faith and hope in the power of medicine.

<u>Why Georgetown University Medical School?</u> My primary motivation to enroll at Georgetown is to acquire a superior medical education in an environment that supports aggressive research on Gaucher Disease and other genetic disorders. Georgetown's affiliation with the University Regional Gaucher Treatment Center will enable me to expand the scope of my current work, which examines gene replacement therapy as a possible cure. Additionally, clinical rotations at Georgetown Medical Center will provide invaluable experience working with a heterogeneous patient base that I would not otherwise encounter.

On an academic basis, I am intrigued by Georgetown's collegial atmosphere, clinical relevancy and exciting yet unconventional teaching methodologies. The inclusion of innovative curricula such as humanism, ethics, preventive care and the Clinical Skills program demonstrates Georgetown's commitment to cooperative learning. In such a nurturing, highly interactive environment, I will forge long-term relationships with mentors and medical practitioners who are renowned for their excellence in research, education and patient care.

As a native of Washington, DC, I am eager to return to the area, where I will be in close proximity to the family, friends and mentors who have encouraged my ambitious goals. Thanks to their support, I feel well prepared for the challenges of a medical career. After evaluating the comparative merits of other programs, I cannot imagine a better place for me than Georgetown. I would be honored to accept an offer of admission.

<u>Our Assessment</u>: This is an exceptional letter from an exceptional candidate who had her heart set on completing her medical degree at Georgetown. This persuasive letter helped her to open that door.

Medical School Waitlist Letter

I was recently placed on the waitlist for Fall 2012 admission to the Temple University School of Medicine. Unfortunately, due to my employment in London, England, I was not able to visit the campus to meet with a member of the admissions committee. During our telephone interview, Dr. Denise Davis encouraged me to keep the committee up-to-date of any new developments in my career. Accordingly, I would like to briefly present the following pieces of additional information: my recent achievements as a public health advocate and my promotion to Department Head at Oxford University.

1. Public Health Advocate. In December of 2011, I was elected President of the British Medical Women's Association (BMWA), which promotes social and professional opportunities for women in medicine. As a clinical psychologist, I am the group's first non-physician President, who brings a decidedly non-technical perspective to the group's agenda. To gain awareness for the group, I have written several newspaper and magazine articles about the human aspects of medicine, including social issues such as sexual abuse, domestic violence, gender issues and medical ethics (see attached copies). I have also given presentations to many social service institutions, including the Juvenile Protection Service and the Center for Refugees from China. A tireless champion of women's rights, I am honored to do my part to promote gender equality in all aspects of society.

Historically, male-dominated professions such as medicine have resisted an open discourse about controversial social and political causes. Consequently, I have been delighted by the overwhelming support I have received from both the public and from leaders of the medical profession. In January of 2012, the British Press named me "Woman of the Year" for my controversial television special, "The past, the present and the future of British women doctors," which revealed blatant inequalities that female physicians encounter in the workplace. Despite the covert pressure from hospital administrators to remain silent, I lobbied strongly for equal pay for women and for equal employment opportunities. Hopefully, with increased public support, the BMWA's efforts will encourage talented women to pursue ambitious and non-traditional career paths.

2. Promotion to Department Head. After working for eight years as a Lecturer in the Department of Women's Health at Oxford University, I was recently promoted to the position of Department Head in the newly-created department of Social & Cultural Anthropology. As a result, I have spent the past six months revising our curriculum to create a separate department that combines all aspects of medical humanities, including medical history, medical ethics, medical sociology and medical anthropology. Although the administrative challenges have been enormous, I am excited by the opportunity to form an interdisciplinary bridge between medicine and anthropology.

By assuming the promotion, I gained valuable leadership experience in an academic setting. I have also flexed my wings and become an expert on diverse aspects of medicine and anthropology. This perspective will be a great asset to my medical school class, as I will bring a wealth of practical experience to classroom discussions on the international aspects of sociology and human behavior.

I appreciate the opportunity to share these recent achievements with the admissions committee. Because of its unparalleled reputation in the academic community, particularly in the area of women's reproductive health, Temple is the perfect place for me to complete my medical education; if granted admission, I will eagerly accept a seat in the class. Please contact me at (phone number) or (email address) if you require additional information.

Our Assessment: This letter, although long and technical, drove home several points that the candidate had failed to include in her personal statement, including her passion for reproductive health and her specific interest in Temple. The letter also showed her excellent writing skills, which made a positive impression on the committee.

Medical School Waitlist Letter

Despite being placed on the waiting list at Harvard Medical School, I am convinced that the program is the ideal place for me to obtain my medical education. Please accept this letter as my intention to enroll if space becomes available in the class.

Aristotle taught us that the path to success in life involves a constant dialogue between hardship and joy, family and career. Over the past year, my experiences have confirmed his teachings. My joy includes:

1. graduating Summa Cum Laude from UCLA with a degree in public health and social services

2. paying my own way through college and graduating with zero debt

3. continuing my rewarding work as a volunteer tutor for learning disabled children at San Marcos Elementary School, where I help my students navigate their way through young adulthood

4. being named 2011's "Volunteer of the Year" for the state of California, and accepting the award from Governor Arnold Schwarzenegger at a ceremony in Sacramento

In contrast, the past year has also brought great hardship, as I lost both of my parents to cancer and faced the emotional strain of selling our family home. My grief, fortunately, was abated by the support of my siblings and my recent academic and community achievements, which represent years of hard work and dedication. After working so hard to fulfill my professional aspirations, I approach the medical school experience with a profound sense of gratitude and optimism.

As I look to the future, I am eager to augment my training in public health with a medical degree to make a more meaningful contribution to my community. As a first step, I recently accepted a position as Interim Director at the San Marcos Center for Children, which is a research and evaluation agency associated with UCLA that fosters youth development through collaborative efforts. The position is for six months and will end just before medical school starts in September. During this time, I will develop a strategy to enable our corporate sponsors to implement their expansive vision.

Before I completed my application to Harvard Medical School, I spoke with professors Harold Greene and Sondra Wyatt, who strongly encouraged me to apply. After supervising my internship at the San Mateo County Child Protective Agency, they felt that my talents and skills were an excellent fit for your program. I am intrigued by the possibilities that Harvard Medical School will offer me, including the chance to lend my skills to the Bernard Koteen Family Clinic.

With the support of your dedicated faculty, I am certain that Harvard will provide a medical education of the highest caliber. If admitted, I will do everything possible to make a lasting contribution to the HMS community.

Our Assessment: Many waitlisted candidates contact the school to update their file, but few do it as powerfully as this applicant, who shed new light on her credentials in this honest and straightforward letter. The committee knew that she would add considerable strength, intelligence, and diversity to their program.

Chapter 10: Final Thoughts

After reading this book, we hope that you feel well-prepared to write your own persuasive medical school personal statement. For best results:

1. Answer the question that was asked.
2. Write naturally, but concisely.
3. Use excellent grammar and punctuation.
4. Show your real personality (let the reader get to know you).
5. Only use humor if it works.
7. Convey a positive message (avoid cynicism).
8. Use the active voice.
9. Be specific and focused / explain events whenever appropriate.
10. Revise and polish until it is perfect.

For additional help in writing and editing letters of recommendation, admissions essays, and personal statements, please visit www.ivyleagueadmission.com.

Remember: in the medical school admissions process, your personal statement can provide the committee with information about your character, motivation and goals that they could not acquire any other way. A well-crafted essay can also explain a variety of personal circumstances (and obstacles) that have affected your performance. By writing a persuasive essay, you will increase your chances of gaining admission to the medical school of your dreams. Don't miss this chance to claim your destiny!

Made in the USA
Lexington, KY
14 February 2017